MW01681073

GROW

VEGETABLES

IN CENTRAL FLORIDA

Rondi Niles

GROWING AND USING VEGETABLES IN RECIPES

Growing Fresh Vegetables in Central Florida

Copyright © 2024 by Rondi Niles

All Rights Reserved. No part of this book may be reproduced in any form or by any electronic or mechanical means including information storage and retrieval systems, without permission in writing from the author. The only exception is by a reviewer, who may quote short excerpts in a review.

Published by Hallard Press LLC. www.HallardPress.com 352.460.6099

Although this publication is designed to provide accurate information in regard to the subject matter covered, the publisher and the author assume no responsibility for errors, inaccuracies, omissions, or any other inconsistencies herein. This publication is meant as a source of valuable information for the reader, however it is not meant as a replacement for direct expert assistance. If such level of assistance is required, the services of a competent professional should be sought.

Library of Congress Control Number: 2024915515

Publisher's Cataloging-in-Publication data

Names: Niles, Rondi

Title: Growing fresh vegetables in Central Florida / Rondi Niles.

Description: The Villages, FL: Hallard Press, LLC, 2024.

Identifiers: LCCN: 2024915515| ISBN: 978-1-962326-41-4 (paperback)
Subjects: LCSH Vegetable gardening – Southern States| Vegetables. | Cooking. | BISAC GARDENING / General | GARDENING / Vegetables | GARDENING / Regional / South (AL, AR, FL, GA, KY, LA, MS, NC, SC, TN, VA, WV)
Classification: LCC SB321.5 .N5 2024 | DDC 635.7--dc23

ISBN: 978-1-962326-41-4 (Paperback)

DEDICATION

This book is dedicated to my husband, Ed, who supported my vegetable growing endeavors by building my beloved greenhouses and large raised bed vegetable garden - complete with beds, drip irrigation, stone paths, white picket fence, and arbors. He also helped tote my vendor tent and all my supplies to the farmers' markets.

He initially considered becoming a chef (though he ultimately went in a different direction). As a result, we have worked together, side-by-side, to create wonderful meals for ourselves and dinner guests throughout the years. And true to form, he helped me cook the recipes in this book. Love him forever.

TABLE OF CONTENTS

PREFACE

With the advent of certain health situations in recent years, growing your own food has made a popular comeback. When stores were closed, and grocery products were flying off the shelves unnaturally, I was grateful to have vegetables growing in my garden right then. Not only is growing a rewarding experience, but it also helps people on their journey to eating better and becoming healthier.

In my professional career as a horticulturist, I grew vegetable plants, starting them from seed in my own greenhouses. I grew many different varieties that I would trial in my huge outdoor vegetable garden. Only the winners would proceed to be planted again the next year.

And those are the ones that I sold at various farmers' markets in New England. I maintained them organically, which resonated with my customers.

However, growing seasons are different here in Florida from what is experienced in other parts of the country. Heat and pests are some of our biggest challenges. As a result, I have also adapted my vegetable-growing practices here. Although I still grow some outdoors, I have moved more towards lanai containers and indoor hydroponics. I share all best practices with you in this book.

My husband and I are also avid cooks, and we have always worked together to host dinner parties, driveway parties, or happy hour gatherings. Included in this book are recipes I have created and made over the years.

Whether you desire to experience more success with growing vegetables in our Central Florida region or you wish to enjoy cooking with vegetables, I hope you find this book a welcome addition to your Floridian growing or cookbook library.

INTRODUCTION

WHY GROW?

There is something about growing your own vegetables. The standing joke is, "I can pay $1 for a tomato in the store, and it costs $3 to grow one on my own." So why do it?

Eating healthy and organically is one popular reason. Preferences exist for plant-based, vegan, or vegetarian diets or just eating food grown without chemicals. These days, grocery stores are getting better at selling different types of vegetables, but finding them organically can sometimes still be challenging.

In New England, farmers' markets were pretty much synonymous with organically grown, and therefore, a good place to find such products. If you went to a cheese booth, it was the actual farmer who milked the cow or goat, selling the cheese that they made. Same with vegetables – it was the actual farms selling their items. But what I discovered in Florida is that it is not necessarily the case. Vegetables may be from a local farm, but they are not necessarily organic. And sometimes products are not even made by the vendor but are merely being resold from who knows where.

Because it can be more difficult growing in Florida, it is probably for that reason that organic practices were limited when I first moved here over a decade ago. Initially, being a snowbird, I would cart all my organic supplies from my home in New England to my house in Florida every year. Thankfully, that has changed, and you can now find a good selection of organic growing products over the internet. Eating organically, without the use of harmful herbicides, pesticides, and synthetic fertilizers, is one of the main reasons to grow your own vegetables.

Another reason is selection. When I first started growing, you could only find red tomatoes in grocery stores, but not yellow, orange, or purple. Creating colorful meals makes them more appealing, and the selection was limited for my culinary palette. Thankfully, that also has changed somewhat. But still, you will not find anywhere near the selection that you can with seed starting and growing yourself. And remember the old adage, "Eat your vegetables?" If you have a family member who is finicky when it comes to vegetables, having newer and more colorful varieties may better appeal to their senses.

Where are your vegetables coming from? The longer it takes for a vegetable to travel from the farmer through the trucking route to your grocery store to your table, the less fresh it becomes. There is no comparison to picking your own vegetables fresh from the garden right before you are ready to eat them. It also saves time from having to run to the grocery store when you decide at the last minute that you want to make a particular dish using vegetables.

Another reason to grow your own is simple – it is a fun and rewarding experience! Growing something from seed and then seeing the results of your labor, something you created, is extremely gratifying. And if you ever worry about another country-wide shutdown, fear no more with your own vegetable "grocery store."

FLORIDA SEASONS

In other states, we grew most vegetables in the summer months, with some cooler crops, like lettuce and spinach, taking advantage of the early spring and fall seasons. Here in Florida, we get an extra growing season - warm crops can be planted for a fall harvest and again for a spring harvest. Little chance of snow or persistent freezes allows cooler crops to over-winter successfully.

And what about summer? Well, that is the difficult part here because it is too hot to grow most crops. The biggest mistake that Florida newcomers make is trying to grow tomatoes in summer, just like they did up north. And just because you happen to find tomato plants available at a garden center in summer, it does not necessarily mean that they will produce.

SMALL SPACE GARDENING

Most existing information on Florida vegetable gardening is concentrated on larger outdoor in-ground gardens. However, many communities in Florida can only support small-scale gardening. And many people, including beginners, those who are busy working, and seniors, do not want the maintenance of an outdoor garden, especially in Florida's sun, heat, and humidity.

Small-space gardening includes container gardening, gardening under screening (birdcages and lanais), and even gardening indoors (especially with hydroponics). Although this book will cover all vegetable gardening aspects, it will feature considerations for manageable container gardening, including under screening.

HOW TO USE THIS BOOK

Now that you are convinced of growing your own or even of just eating more healthy vegetables, let us get started.

This book is divided into three sections. The first part explains how to grow vegetables in Central Florida in general. The second part covers the specifics of the most popular vegetables, broken down by season, with a quick reference chart at the end of each. The third part is a compilation of my favorite recipes that I have created and used over my many years of cooking and entertaining.

PART 1 – GROWING VEGETABLES

GARDEN LOCATIONS

The first step is to locate where your vegetable garden will be placed, and there are several considerations for our Central Florida area.

OUTDOORS

If you have the space in your yard, you can create an outdoor garden. An advantage is that you will probably be able to grow more vegetables compared to other locations that may require containers. The disadvantage of outdoor gardens is that your vegetables will be more susceptible to weeds, animals, insects, and soil-borne diseases. And these seem to be more prevalent in Florida than in northern parts of our country. Overall, outdoor gardens are more work.

Outdoor gardens are usually created via raised beds to best handle our severe rains and allow for drainage. Beds should be 4 feet or less in width so you can maintain and harvest without stepping on and compacting the soil. If you must have a pathway inside a bed, use stepping stones for walking on. Cedar wood is good to use because it is more durable via natural preservatives rather than being treated with chemicals and is somewhat termite resistant. You can also buy kits, which contain all the parts and make assembly easy. Kit sides are made from cedar, metal, or composite materials.

Stone is another way to build your outdoor beds and make them last longer than wood.

Due to our abundance of beautiful weather, patios are prevalent in Florida. If you do not have room for an in-ground garden, patios are ideal for container vegetable gardening.

SCREENED BIRDCAGES AND LANAIS

A birdcage is a screened-in area without a roof, usually found over pools, but also can merely enclose patios and gardens; this is called a serenity birdcage. Birdcages are subject to the outside elements of sun, rain, temperature, humidity, and wind.

Lanais are screened-in areas under a roof, like screened-in porches found in other areas of the country. Although under cover, they may still be subject to many of the same outside elements, such as rain blowing in. Depending on which direction a lanai faces, the amount of sun that plants receive may vary, a major consideration if growing full-sun plants.

It is a myth that growing under screening will prevent insect damage. The screening will indeed prevent larger pests from getting to your crops. However, it will not stop smaller insects from going through the screen. And you are apt to find more of them than if you were growing outdoors, where the larger pests eat the smaller ones and keep them in check. The screening also will not prevent diseases.

Another factor is what type of crop you are growing. Bees and other pollinators cannot get through the screen to do their job if needed.

INDOORS

Florida rooms, like sunrooms in other parts of the country, are under the cover of a roof and enclosed in glass. The benefit to growing indoors is that you have control over temperature, humidity, and, best of all, pests. However, it can be tough to grow larger vegetable plants indoors unless you have the appropriate amount of space. And how much sun you get is also a consideration, sometimes hard to get indoors. You can use grow lights, but they are more practical for smaller and part-shade crops (like lettuce). And, same as under screening, pollinators cannot do their job.

POLLINATION CONSIDERATIONS

Whether your crop needs pollination and how much pollination is needed will affect where you can locate your vegetable plants/garden.

It is the age-old question - is the tomato a vegetable or a fruit? Whatever your guess, you would be correct. Botanically, any "vegetable" that has a seed is technically a fruit. Tomatoes, peppers, cucumbers, beans, and more fall into that category, whereas lettuce, for example, does not. Legally, however, it is classified as a vegetable. This was the result of a Supreme Court ruling back in 1893 where farmers were being taxed on vegetables, and they argued that tomatoes and such were actually fruits and, therefore, should be exempt from taxation. They lost the case – for taxation purposes, they were deemed to be vegetables.

So, how does that affect the topic of pollination? Crops that produce fruits need pollination. There are several methods of pollination:

- ***Insects.*** Squash and most cucumbers are examples of vegetables with separate male and female structures that need insects to perform pollination. Interestingly, when we think of pollinators, we usually think of bees, but there are other flying insects that do the job, too. You cannot grow vegetable plants under screening or glass if they require insect pollination.

Bee on African Basil

- ***Wind.*** Corn is an example of a crop that is wind-pollinated. The top tassel on each plant contains the male pollen, and each ear has female silk. The wind is enough to perform the pollination between the pollen and silk. So, although somewhat impractical, you could grow ears of corn on your lanai as long as your lanai occasionally gets windy.
- ***Self-pollinating.*** Here is the surprise! Most tomatoes, peppers, and beans have male and female structures on the same flower and pollinate themselves - no insects needed! Below is proof - a photo of my hydroponic system in my lanai with a plant fully loaded with tomatoes. However, there are exceptions, which we will cover next.

HEIRLOOMS VERSUS HYBRIDS

Two types of seeds are used, and these will also affect where you place your vegetable plants/garden.

- ***Heirloom.*** These are "open-pollinated," meaning they need insect pollination. If you are trying to grow heirloom tomatoes, you must grow them outside. It can be tough to grow heirlooms in Florida because heirlooms are generally more susceptible to pests and diseases. One technique you may find in stores is grafted plants, whereby heirloom plants are grafted onto a stronger rootstock, allowing for the flavor of heirloom fruits but with the better disease handling of hybrids. If you are planning to save seeds from year to year, you will need to grow heirlooms.
- ***Hybrid.*** Hybrids were bred with advantageous traits, including the ability to handle disease resistance. Because our Floridian climate causes more diseases, hybrids are more successfully grown here than heirlooms. Most seeds sold these days are hybrids. That means you can grow hybrid varieties of tomatoes, peppers, cucumbers, and more under screening or indoors.

POLLINATION TIPS

Sometimes, vegetable plants on lanais are not producing fruit, and someone may insist that a lack of pollination is the cause. That is not always correct since there are other reasons plants may not bear fruit. For instance, tomatoes will not flower if temperatures are too high. If the fertilizer being used has too much nitrogen, the plant will put its energy into leaf development at the expense of producing flowers. Too much rain may knock off the blossoms. Or the plant may just be done with its natural growing cycle (for example, determinate tomatoes, discussed later).

Even though self-pollinating crops do not need insects to set fruit, they will produce more fruits if pollinated with other plants (blueberries are the same way). Just because a self-pollinating vegetable plant does not need pollination, it doesn't mean that it won't accept pollination. If growing outdoors, this will happen automatically via insects and wind.

If growing under screening or indoors, you can increase pollination and fruiting yourself. Commercial greenhouse growers, growing under cover, shake the plants to increase pollination. Or place your containers where they can get some wind. Many of us in Florida have lanais, and they usually have an overhead fan – turn it on! You can also try misting the flowers, particularly with warm water.

Greens and rooting crops do not need pollination for us to eat them. (However, they may need pollination to produce seed, if you will be seed-saving.)

GROWING METHODS

If not utilizing an in-ground garden, you will need something to grow your vegetables in. These can be containers or hydroponic/aeroponic systems.

CONTAINERS

Growing in containers has some advantages. Outside containers can be temporarily moved inside in a cold snap. Some vegetables are better with afternoon shade, and containers can be moved around seasonally as the sun moves. Soil-borne pests and diseases are lessened. They are also smaller and thus easier to maintain than an outdoor garden. And they can be placed close to a kitchen door for ready harvesting.

However, the container mix will need to be amended each season, just like an outdoor garden, and will need replacing over time as air pockets for roots become compressed from watering.

Containers are made from many different materials. The most popular ones are plastic because they are lightweight, weather-resistant, and long-lasting. They also come in many pleasing styles and colors, especially if you care about aesthetics. (Notice my red containers for tomatoes in the photo!) If they do not have a drainage hole, you will need to drill some, but it is easily done with plastic. You can also find containers with wheels and even built-in trellises.

Container size needs are typically underestimated. It may look like a small plant initially, but it will grow! A round container at least 12-14" in diameter and 12" deep is needed for most tomatoes, peppers, cucumbers, and other larger vegetable plants or root crops that need depth.

Carol's elevated container garden

Elevated box containers with legs (photo on left) and vertical containers (photo on right) are becoming more popular because they assist ergonomically - easier to plant and harvest without having to bend over. Some are shallower and best for smaller plants and herbs, but depth can vary, so be sure to get one deep enough for whatever vegetables you plan on growing.

Karen's vertical grow garden

Another type of container is a grow bag made from permeable fabric that allows for good aeration and drainage. They are economical and can be folded flat for storage in between seasons. Many vegetable crops can be grown in them, and I have grown potatoes with success (which makes "hilling" easier, discussed later).

Self-watering containers may be used, depending on where and when you are using them and what kind you buy. They tend to be more expensive than regular containers. They have a reservoir full of water on the bottom that is wicked up into the soil as it dries out, keeping the soil consistently moist. This is a plus for shallow-rooted vegetables or those that need regular moisture (which is the case for most vegetables). Moisture assists with nutrient uptake. The reservoir will need to be filled every so often, but it cuts down on watering chores overall and helps if you will be away from home for a bit.

They work especially well for plants kept under cover or outdoors in our dry season. However, they do not allow for drainage, and particularly if used outdoors during our humid and rainy season in Florida, they may keep the soil too wet. In that case, be sure to get a model that has an overflow hole so excess moisture can be released. And be sure to keep the fill/overflow hole unclogged from debris and watch for mosquitoes entering.

HYDROPONICS

Hydroponics means plants are grown in water ("hydro") instead of soil. The plants are suspended in net pots or expanded clay pebbles, with their roots in water all or part of the time. The water should be aerated to mix in the oxygen needed for plant roots.

Typically, hydroponic units are used indoors or under cover. If indoors, crops can be grown year-round. Plants are fed via a nutrient solution that is regularly added to the water, which may result in faster-growing plants. Another advantage to hydroponic growing is that soil-borne diseases are eliminated, certain pests (those that breed in soil) may be reduced, and there is no weeding involved.

Hydroponic units come in different models. I have a smaller one on my countertop, where the roots are continually in water, aerated by a timer to bring in the necessary oxygen.

I have a larger one in my Florida room which is called an ebb and flow model. This has two containers, one inserted on top of the other. The water is held in the bottom container and periodically via a timer uses a pump to push the water into the top growing container. This wets the roots for about 20 minutes, and then the water drains back into the bottom container.

AEROPONICS

Aeroponics is like hydroponics in that plants are not grown in soil. However, unlike hydroponics, plant roots hang in the air ("aero") and are occasionally misted with water. Aeroponics is said to be even faster growing since more oxygen gets to the roots. Same as hydroponics, plants are fed via a nutrient system, and you will need to monitor the pH in these systems, as well as potentially refreshing with clean water. They may be used outdoors but are usually located indoors or under cover.

Aeroponic systems tend to be much more expensive than hydroponic, and it is important to place plants in proper size order, with smaller plants on top and larger ones on the bottom, so that all roots get misted adequately and the sun reaches all plants.

WHICH METHOD IS BETTER?

Which is better—hydroponics or aeroponics? I personally do not find one to be better than the other, but that could just be my experience.

Which is better—hydroponics/aeroponics or containers? The former requires more work with feeding and keeping the systems clean. However, containers are more prone to pests and diseases. I typically grow larger vegetables in containers, and smaller ones hydroponically. When I get tired of the hydroponic maintenance, I take a break and switch back to containers.

GARDEN DESIGN

These design techniques are especially important for planning a successful in-ground garden. Some also apply to containers.

CROP ROTATION

This technique involves planting your crops in different locations each year. Vegetables fall into different botanical families, with each family having similar attributes. For example, tomatoes, peppers, and eggplant are all in the same family, and crop rotation is usually done by family, meaning that for crop rotation purposes, they are treated the same.

One purpose is to help with soil recovery. For instance, night-shade family crops such as tomatoes and peppers utilize a lot of nutrients in the soil while growing. Planting those locations the following year with peas or beans instead, which are nitrogen-fixing crops, will help the soil recover from being depleted.

Rotating can also help foil pests and diseases. For instance, squash is prone to squash bug damage, but moving the squash the following year to a new location makes it more difficult for the bug to find your squash again.

There are still considerations, however, that will impact your ability to rotate everything. One is your sun location. Smaller crops should be planted in the front of the garden, with larger ones in the back. You may have to move the smaller crops in one rotation grouping, and larger ones in a different rotation. If you have any vegetable plants that are perennials (kept from year to year), they will have to stay where they are initially placed, and your other crops rotated around those.

You can see how this is done from the chart I created for my 50′ x 50′ in-ground garden. I would modify it every year when designing my rotations for that year's garden.

The larger the garden, the more successful rotating will be. If you are using containers and are having a problem with pests, you can move your containers to a different area of your yard.

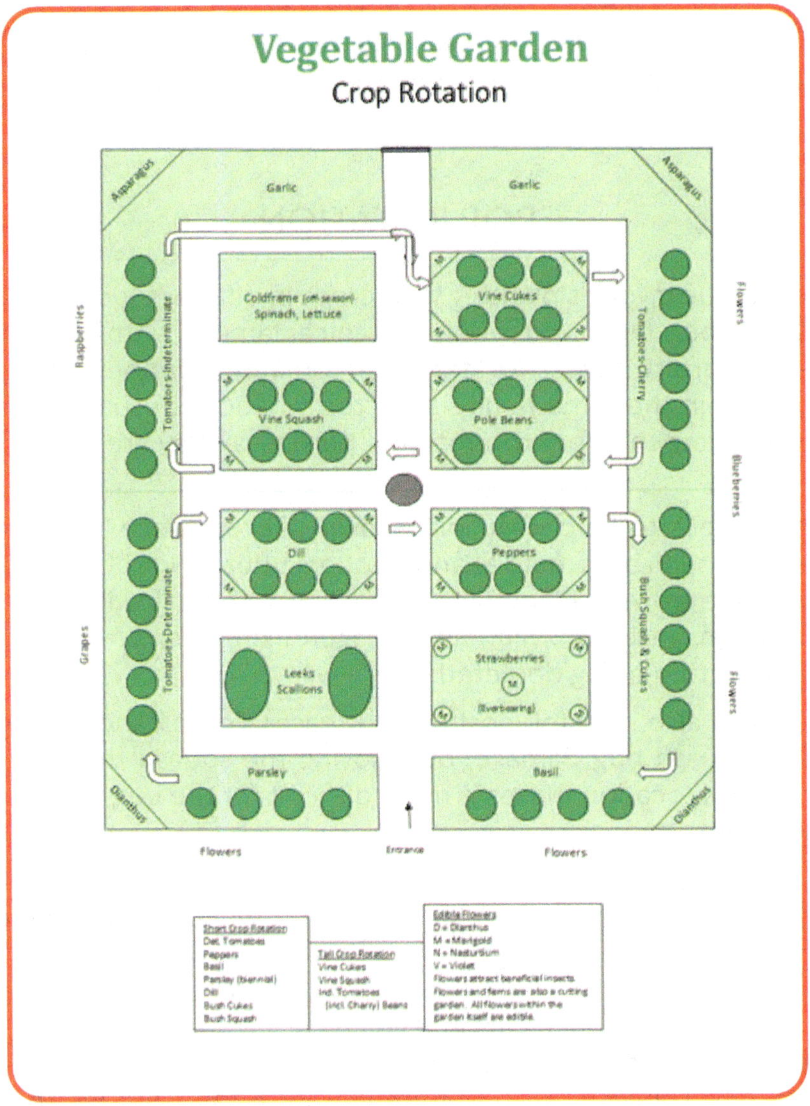

INTERPLANTING

Interplanting is a technique whereby different vegetables (or other edible plants), are planted amongst each other.

There are several ways and purposes of interplanting. One is to help confuse pests. This example shows scallions planted throughout the other cold-weather plants.

The example at right is a container filled with lettuce, herbs, and edible flowers.

A space-saving example is when a quicker-growing vegetable that matures first, like lettuce, is planted with a slower vegetable plant, like a tomato. The tomato is small at first, so lettuce primarily consumes the garden or container space. As the weather gets warmer and the tomato grows, it helps provide shade to the lettuce. By the time the lettuce is harvested and removed, the tomato has grown large enough and can utilize the space unto itself.

Another famous example is the "three sisters," whereby corn, squash, and beans are planted closely together. The beans use the corn as a trellis, as well as fixing the nitrogen in the soil that the corn uses heavily. Since corn is beloved by raccoons and other critters, the squash, which can be prickly, surrounds the base of the corn and keeps them away. It also provides a living mulch and suppresses weeds around the corn and beans. It is a win-win for all the crops involved!

INTENSIVE GARDENING

This technique involves making the most of your limited space by growing crops closely together. It intersperses crops with different root depths, plant heights, and growth rates. It concentrates resources, such as water, fertilizer, and compost, in that one space. The benefit is that it uses less space and requires less weeding. One example is known as square foot gardening, which uses blocks of crops planted densely in squares, instead of spaced-out rows. This can be implemented in containers also.

SUCCESSION PLANTING

Succession planting means not planting a crop all at once, but rather in successive cycles. This is good to do in containers also. There are two methods that accomplish different goals.

One is successive plantings, about two weeks part, of a single crop. For example, planting a single row of lettuce in week one, then another row two weeks later, and so forth. That way you will always have a steady stream of new lettuce, rather than having all heads mature at one time and being impossible to eat!

The second method helps with the space management of multiple crops. For example, you can grow quick-growing cold-season radishes, and after they are harvested, the space can be used for warm-season tomatoes. The example shown is a photo of a cool-season bed that will eventually be used for warm-season vegetables.

GROWING VERTICALLY

Using stakes to grow vining vegetable plants vertically serves two purposes. The first is that it saves space, by growing up rather than rambling out. You will be able to grow more of a given crop.

The second is that the plant and fruit are up off the soil, which reduces the chance of disease. For example, there are bush-type squash and cucumbers, but the vining types are typically grown vertically.

COMPANION PLANTING

Companion planting is the notion that plants can have a synergistic relationship, planted together for beneficial purposes. Some examples are below.

- ***Flowers*** can be planted amongst vegetables to attract pollinators and predatory insects. They also make a garden pretty. If using containers, you can plant flowers alongside your vegetable plants within a single container, or have a separate container of flowers nearby.

A cutting garden outside the garden will also accomplish this. And you can have flowers as a centerpiece for your table!

- ***Marigolds*** repel root-knot nematodes in the soil. And the fragrance can repel aphids from peppers.
- ***Garlic*** has fungicidal properties which protect tomatoes and potatoes from blights. It also may confuse beetles attracted to the scent of cucumbers. And the smell can repel rabbits.

- ***Trap crop*** plants attract pests, thereby keeping them away from desirable crops. Nasturtiums and radishes, for example, attract aphids, keeping them away from tomatoes.
- ***Allelopathic*** plants, such as those in the cabbage family, can prevent the growth of nearby plants. Solanaceous family crops (tomatoes, etc.) are most susceptible, so do not plant them together with cabbage.

Companion planting can have mixed results. It is not always scientifically based, but sometimes may be folklore that has just not been proven yet. Reference online studies to find the most accurate and up-to-date information.

Also, results may vary by year, such as whether the environment experienced drought conditions or perhaps it was extra hot. Success rates can even vary by different gardens in a neighborhood since soil conditions and more are different from one garden to the next. Keep records of what works best for your garden.

SEEDING AND BUYING

Most vegetable plants are annuals, meaning they only last one season and are, therefore, planted anew each year. Most annual plants are started from seed. You can do it yourself, or you can buy already growing plants from a garden center, which in turn were bought from a grower who did the initial seeding.

BUYING SEED PACKETS

Big box stores or local nurseries will have seed packets for the most popular vegetables. However, for the best selection of different varieties, you may wish to order from online seed companies. The best time to order is by early January before the newer varieties get sold out. It is always fun to pour through the catalogs and select the latest options.

As far as which varieties of crops to grow in Florida, do not rely solely on online articles or books for "best varieties for Florida." Articles can be outdated, and although older varieties will still do well, newer varieties are always being developed. This is particularly true for tomatoes, for which there have been significant breeding advances. Instead, look for descriptions such as "heat tolerant," "humidity tolerant," "bred for southern disease tolerance," or "bred in/for Florida."

Also, pay attention to the marketing description. Tomatoes, for example, can be described as "sweet" or "stores well." The latter sacrifices some taste for being able to stay on store shelves longer.

Some seeds come with enhancements. For instance, corn sometimes comes with a fungicide coating (typically not organic) to protect it initially in the soil. You may have heard that legumes (peas, beans) need inoculation with nitrogen-fixing bacteria, but that is generally not needed in Florida due to our native strains of bacteria. Some seeds are organic, but it is more important how you raise your crops than the seed itself.

Some crops do not use normal seeds. Onions use sets, garlic uses bulb cloves, and potatoes use the eyes, for example. You are more likely to find these at local farm stores, but if you order online, just be sure to order varieties meant for Central Florida.

SEED STORAGE

Store your seed packets in a cool, dry place. Since most homes in Florida have air conditioning, inside your home is fine. Commercial growers will keep them in refrigerators, which keep them healthy even longer.

The seed packet should have a date for when the seeds were packed. Seeds will generally last at least 2-3 years after that date, but some will last even longer. To test viability, place a few seeds in a glass of water for a couple of hours. If they have sunk, they are good, but if they are still floating, they are not.

WHEN TO SEED

You can "direct seed," which means placing seeds directly into your outdoor garden soil or container (this is sometimes done with crops that are more difficult to transplant). But usually, seeding is first done indoors to get a jump start on the growing season.

Check your seed packet or the marketing description for germination time. Starting with the correct time of year to plant for Central Florida (for spring warm-weather crops, this is known as the last frost date), then subtract germination time for a given crop to determine when you should seed.

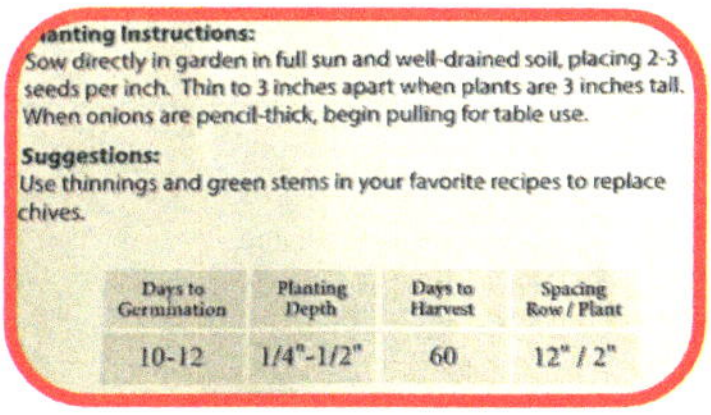

anting Instructions:
Sow directly in garden in full sun and well-drained soil, placing 2-3 seeds per inch. Thin to 3 inches apart when plants are 3 inches tall. When onions are pencil-thick, begin pulling for table use.

Suggestions:
Use thinnings and green stems in your favorite recipes to replace chives.

Days to Germination	Planting Depth	Days to Harvest	Spacing Row / Plant
10-12	1/4"-1/2"	60	12" / 2"

Or you can use this cheat sheet for the most popular vegetables. I originally made this chart for growing in New England, and have since modified it based on my experience in Florida. Note that since different crop seeds mature at different speeds, you will need to plant seeds at different times as well if you want them all to be ready for planting out at the same time.

FL Seed Starting & Planting Guide		
Season/Crop	**Seed Indoors**	**Ready for Transplant**
Fall (Warm)		
Peppers	early July	8 wks
Tomatoes	mid July	6 wks
Cukes, Squash, Melon, Corn	late July	4 wks
Winter (Cool - seed continually)		
Lettuce, Radishes	mid-Sept	4 wks
Scallions	mid-Sept	4 wks
Spinach	mid-Sept	4 wks
Spring (Warm: Last frost date mid-Mar)		
Peppers	early Jan	8 wks
Tomatoes	mid-Jan	6 wks
Cukes, Squash, Melon, Corn	late Jan	4 wks
Summer (Hot)		
Cherry Tomatoes	late Mar	6 wks

FL Seed Starting & Planting Guide		
Plant Outdoors	**Days to Harvest**	**Harvest Done**
late Aug	60-80	late Nov
late Aug	75-90	late Nov
late Aug	40-50	late Nov
mid-Oct thru Mar	40-70	early-mid Mar
mid-Oct thru Feb	30-40	early-mid Mar
mid-Oct thru Mar	45-60	early-mid Mar
early Mar	60-80	early June
early Mar	75-90	early June
early Mar	40-50	early June
late May	75-90	good luck!

Look at the example below. I started all these seeds at the same time for demonstration purposes, and you can see the progress made each week by crop. Note that lettuce is the fastest growing, followed by tomatoes, then peppers—hence, the reason pepper seeds are planted two weeks before tomato seeds in order to plant both crops outdoors at the same time.

LETTUCE

Week 1

Week 2

Week 3

Week 4

TOMATOES

Week 1

Week 2

Week 3

Week 4

PEPPERS

Week 1

Week 2

Week 3

Week 4

You may have heard of planting by the phases of the moon. Above-ground crops (ex., tomatoes) are planted outdoors on a waxing (new to full) moon to gravitationally encourage upward growth. Root crops (ex., potatoes) are planted on a waning (full to new) moon. Is it merely a woo-woo, new-age concept, or is there any validity to it? Scientific opinion questions it, but some farmers swear by it. I have indeed tried it, but I'm not sure it made any difference.

SEEDING CONTAINERS

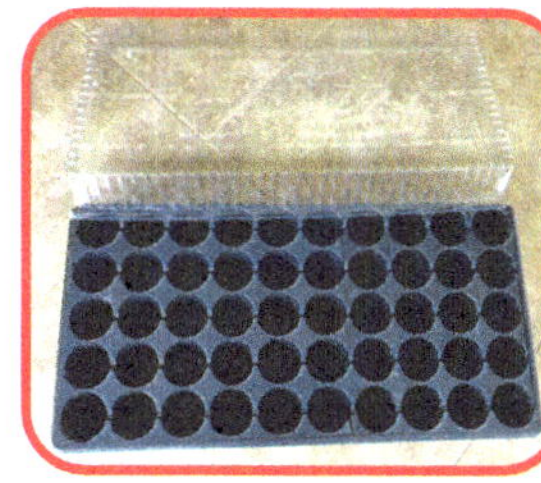

For seeding indoors, if growing multiple plants and/or crops, you will want to start with a setup that includes a tray, cell pack, and clear dome.

If you are only doing one or two plants, you can start with individual small pots, 3 inches or less. These can be black plastic grower pots, peat pots, peat pellet pots, homemade blocks, cups, etc. I have tried them all, but I find cell packs to be the easiest overall. Peat pots are good for certain vegetable plants that have a reputation as being more difficult to transplant because you can plant them directly in the ground, pot and all.

Grower pot

Peat pot

Peat Pellet

Place your pots in a tray. You will also need plastic wrap to mimic a dome over each pot.

Do not, however, start with a single tray when mixing a variety of plants. When the seedlings are ready to be removed, the roots will have grown together and could rip, causing damage to the plants. Also, the time-frame for crop readiness will be set back by 2-3 weeks.

SEEDING MIXES

Seeding mixes are different than regular container mixes in that they are more lightweight.

There are several popular brands with slightly different ingredients. They all start with peat moss or coir (coconut husks) as the base, with perlite or vermiculite added for drainage. From there, you may find additions such as fertilizer, limestone to adjust pH, mycorrhizal fungi, or a wetting agent.

(You can find a more detailed description of these ingredients in the Planting section.)

They all have their advantages, but I personally have found coir (see photo) to hold more moisture than peat moss, which can be the death of seedlings if you are not careful with your watering. And I prefer to add my own organic fertilizer rather than using the one that may come with a mix. A wetting agent is usually not organic. But if using a mix without it, you will have to add water and knead or soak the mix first to get it to absorb water until it is slightly damp. Do this before filling your trays.

SEEDING STEPS

STEP 1 – FILL WITH MIX.

Fill your cells with the seedling mix. Press down lightly with two fingers. Add additional mix, if necessary, until it is a half inch from the top.

STEP 2 – LABEL.

Label each cell, or each row of cells if all the same plant in a row. Labels may have to be cut in half so that they will fit under the dome. You will find wooden or plastic varieties. Wooden can sometimes soak up the water and eventually prevent being able to read it. For that reason, I prefer the plastic ones. Writing with a permanent marker is best. Label before you plant! Otherwise, once you have placed the seed, you may forget what seed was where. (How do I know this?!)

STEP 3 – PLACE SEEDS.

For larger seeds, like tomatoes, create a hole in the center of each cell. Most seeds need to be about ¼" deep, but verify with your seed packet for correct planting depth. Place larger seeds in the hole and close up the hole.

Alternatively, you can place the larger seeds on top of the soil, gently push them into the soil to the appropriate depth, and cover the hole. For tiny seeds (like carrots), spread a few seeds on top of the mix in the cell, then add additional mix to lightly cover. Some seeds (such as lettuce) need light to germinate and, therefore, should not be covered at all or else covered very lightly with mix. Check your specific seed packet instructions.

To ensure germination, two seeds may be planted per cell; this is called "overseeding." Some seeds naturally have a poorer germination rate, and your seed packet should note that. Another reason to overseed is if your seeds are getting older. If both did successfully germinate, one will eventually need to be removed. You could also just seed an extra cell or two, but that is wasting mix if it does not germinate.

There are some tools you may find handy. You can use a "dibble," a stick of some sort, for creating your holes, especially handy when planting many seeds. (You can also use the pointy end of a label.) A pair of long tweezers can pick up seeds that went astray instead of into the hole.

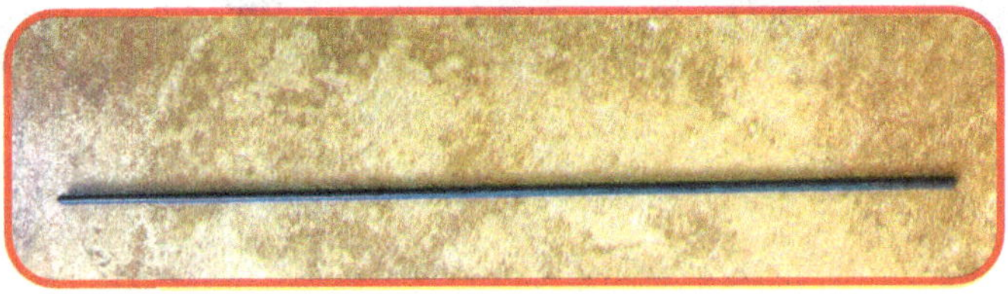

Dibble

If you are planting many seeds, you can buy a vibrating seeder tool. A number of seeds get loaded into it, and then it vibrates so that one seed comes off at a time as you move from cell to cell. It is a more expensive tool, but very worth it if you are doing a lot of seeding. I purchased one years ago when growing for selling, and I still use it to this day.

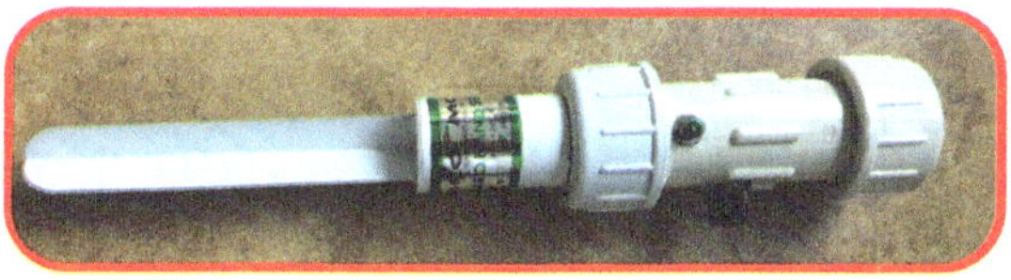

Vibrating seeder

Some seeds (such as scallions) have a hard seed coating and will take longer to germinate. The seeds can be soaked overnight to speed germination. Larger seeds, like nasturtium, can be nicked slightly with a knife prior to planting.

STEP 4 – COVER.

Cover your tray with the clear dome. If you do not have a dome, or are using individual pots, cover with plastic wrap. This helps keep the soil moist for germination. Professional growers do not use domes but rather have automatic misting systems.

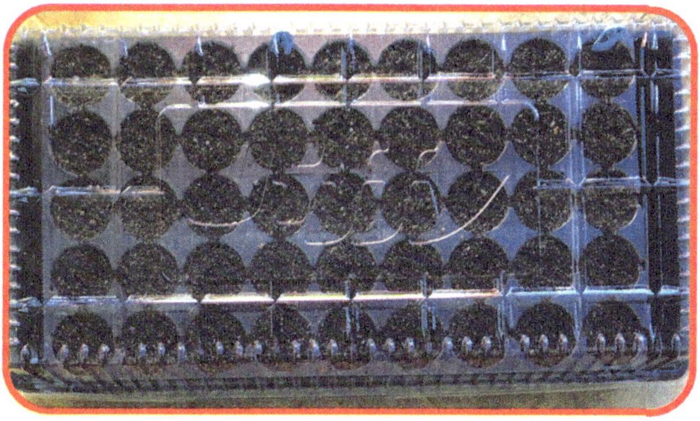

Check regularly to ensure that the soil is still slightly moist, but do not overwater it. Too much water could result in damping off disease, which turns the stem at the soil line black, rotting and killing the seedling. Bottom watering from the tray is best, letting the water soak up into the cell soil as needed. If you have overwatered, take the dome or plastic off immediately.

STEP 5 – HEATING MATS.

Heating mats decrease germination time, particularly for warm-season vegetables. Unless you have planted late and are in a hurry, or you are attempting to grow in a cold location in your home, you probably do not need these in Central Florida. They will be detrimental to cold weather crops, which need cooler temperatures to germinate. I found this out the hard way one year when I used heating mats for my lettuce seeds, and very few germinated. You can place your tray on top of a warm refrigerator also, just until the seeds germinate, as long as the seeds do not need light to germinate.

STEP 6 - LIGHTING.

Place your tray under grow lights for best results. Grow lights for plants are full-spectrum and work best. They are more expensive, so regular florescent shop lights will work also. There are also many inexpensive mini-models available these days. You can try a sunny window instead if need be, but many people seem to have more difficulty with this.

Grow lights are not as strong as the sun. They need to be kept on a timer for 14-16 hours per day. Place your tray so that it is 2-3 inches below the light.

As the seedlings emerge and grow taller, move the light up, but always keep the light that same distance above the plants. This will create stronger stems. (Another reason why it can be harder growing in a window.)

I once went away for a few days and left my seedlings to germinate. When I came back, to my horror, they had indeed germinated, but they were flopping all over the place. It turned out that our electricity had gone out, and the lights never came back on. Once I got the lights working again, within a week the seedlings had recovered. But it shows what happens to seedlings without necessary light.

Light loss

Light restored

GERMINATION

The seed, tiny as it is, contains everything necessary to produce the first baby or seed leaves, called cotyledons. These leaves usually look quite different from the "true" leaves that appear afterward.

Cotyledon leaves on tomato

True leaves on tomato

If you overseeded and got two seedlings to germinate in a cell or pot, now is the time to thin them out. At the soil line, cut the stem of what appears to be the weaker of the two seedlings. This is done with scissors or pruners. Do not pull it out since it will disturb the roots of the little seedling that is left.

Once the true leaves have appeared, remove the dome or plastic. Also, remove the heating mat. The mat helps with germination, but once that has occurred, it can actually hinder creation of a strong stem.

SEEDLING CARE

Besides providing adequate water and light, there are a couple of other ways to encourage strong plants. One way is to regularly touch the plants, gently brushing them back and forth. It is not pseudo-science, it actually works!

When I was in horticulture school, we did a lab experiment where we had pots of marigold seedlings that we planted from seed and placed next to each other, with the same lighting and misting conditions in the greenhouse. The only difference was that throughout the semester, we gently brushed the seedlings in half of the pots and used the other half as a control. Sure enough, the stems were stronger (wider, more compact) on the ones we brushed. The scientific name for this is thigmomorphogenesis, which is the response by plants to mechanical stimuli that, in turn, alter their growth patterns.

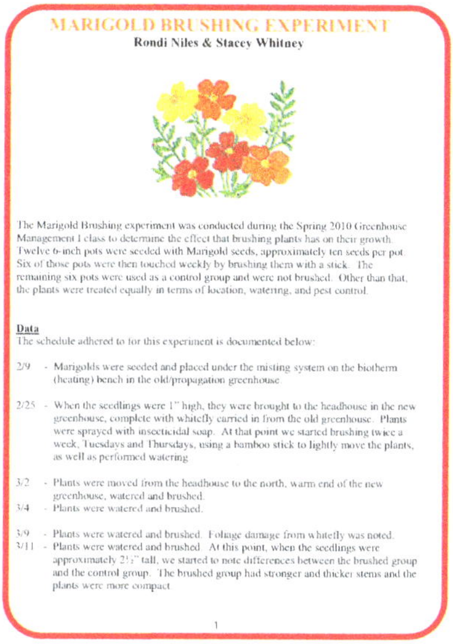

MARIGOLD BRUSHING EXPERIMENT

Rondi Niles & Stacey Whitney

The Marigold Brushing experiment was conducted during the Spring 2010 Greenhouse Management I class to determine the effect that brushing plants has on their growth. Twelve 6-inch pots were seeded with Marigold seeds, approximately ten seeds per pot. Six of those pots were then touched weekly by brushing them with a stick. The remaining six pots were used as a control group and were not brushed. Other than that, the plants were treated equally in terms of location, watering, and pest control.

Data

The schedule adhered to for this experiment is documented below:

2/9 - Marigolds were seeded and placed under the misting system on the biotherm (heating) bench in the old/propagation greenhouse.

2/25 - When the seedlings were 1" high, they were brought to the headhouse in the new greenhouse, complete with whitefly carried in from the old greenhouse. Plants were sprayed with insecticidal soap. At that point we started brushing twice a week, Tuesdays and Thursdays, using a bamboo stick to lightly move the plants, as well as performed watering.

3/2 - Plants were moved from the headhouse to the north, warm end of the new greenhouse, watered and brushed.

3/4 - Plants were watered and brushed.

3/9 - Plants were watered and brushed. Foliage damage from whitefly was noted.

3/11 - Plants were watered and brushed. At this point, when the seedlings were approximately 2½" tall, we started to note differences between the brushed group and the control group. The brushed group had stronger and thicker stems and the plants were more compact.

1

Another way to strengthen stems is to run a gentle fan nearby. Professional growers generally have fans running in their greenhouses.

And what about talking to your plants? There is indeed scientific evidence that plants understand you - not your words per se, but your energy and intentions. So be a cheerleader for your vegetable plants!

UPSIZING

Once two sets of true leaves have appeared, verify that you have a strong set of roots. At that point, it is time to plant.

Professional growers will pot up 3"-5" pots for market, and that is typically how you would buy a plant at the store. You, too, can do this intermediate step if your plants are ready earlier than you are able to plant in their final destination.

Upsized tomato plants

Upsized cucumber plants

BUYING VEGETABLE PLANTS

Are there advantages to buying plants instead of seeding them yourself? Obviously, seeding takes a bit more work, although most would call it fun, whereas you can buy plants that are ready to go. However, you will not find a selection of different varieties that you can with seeds. And would you really want to miss the anticipation of new seed catalogs coming out around the holidays with next year's latest and greatest new varieties?

Is eating organically important to you? Many commercial growers who sell to big box stores and garden centers do not grow plants organically. You may have better luck with a smaller grower, such as either at a farmers' market or local plant fair.

When buying vegetable plants from a garden center or big box store, make sure it is the proper growing season for that crop. Stores will keep vegetable plants around on their shelves until they sell. It is not uncommon to find leftover tomato plants in the heat of summer, for example, but you probably will not get many tomatoes as a result.

Be sure to check the quality of the plant. Inspect the leaves for insects and shake the plant gently to see if any fly away. Big box stores and some garden centers do not spray for pests, perhaps because pesticide applicators must be licensed, a specialized skillset. Also, look at the bottom of the pot to see if roots are growing out of it, in which case the plant is already root-bound and will need some disentangling before planting, which can reduce the success rate.

PLANTING STEPS

Now that you have bought or created seedlings, it is time to plant them outdoors or in your final container.

PLANTING TIMEFRAME

Make sure you are planting at the right time for either the warm or cool season. In spring, it is common to be anxious to plant earlier than you really should, before our last frost date. If you do plant earlier, watch temperatures, and if expecting a frost, use frost blankets to cover your crops overnight. If using containers, move them inside for the night. You can also water your crops the night before, which helps retain heat in the soil.

HARDENING OFF

Your baby vegetable plants will need to be acclimated slowly to outdoor environmental conditions before planting. This process is called "hardening off" and gets the plants used to wind, temperature changes, rain, and direct sun (especially if you use grow lights, which are weaker than the sun).

Start by moving your grower pots outdoors for one hour the first day and then bringing them back inside. On the second day, put them out for two hours, and so forth, until you reach a full day outside (in other words, over about a week's time). If you start to see white spots on the leaves, it is most likely sunburn, and you should slow down the process.

Purchased plants are probably already hardened off from being outside at the store, but not always. It depends on what the grower initially did with them, how long they have been sitting on the store shelves, and whether they are under garden center shade cloths.

PREPPING YOUR IN-GROUND GARDEN SOIL

If you are creating raised beds for the first time or need additional soil because pulling out plants at year-end leaves holes, you can buy a mix meant for vegetable outdoor/in-ground gardens. It will typically be a local product meant for our area and be comprised of peat, sand, and compost.

Native Floridian soil has a large portion of sand, which is wonderful because of its excellent drainage. But for growing vegetables, you will need to add some compost every 2-3 years because it dissipates over time, especially with our porous soil and rains in Central Florida.

If you are utilizing an in-ground garden, it is recommended that you get your soil tested. Your local county extension office can tell you how to do this and where to send your sample. Testing will provide your pH levels. Vegetables grow best in a pH of 5.8 to 6.3, slightly acidic, but most will do okay slightly beyond that range. It is hard to amend your soil to adjust pH levels (especially if too alkaline), but adding compost can help.

Test each year prior to planting, at least until you understand how many nutrients are being depleted annually for your particular environment and crops. Farmers sometimes use cover crops, which are planted after a field is done, to help replenish the soil.

You will also need to prep by adding fertilizer, which is discussed in another section below.

FILLING YOUR CONTAINER

Cover the drainage hole of your container with landscape fabric or a coffee filter to prevent the mix from coming out. Landscape fabric will last a long time, but comes in large rolls and is more expensive. Coffee filters break down quicker, but by the time they do, the mix is usually settled from watering anyway. Fill your container initially to 1″ below the container rim. After planting, you may need to add additional mix.

Use a mix specifically formulated as either a "potting" or "container" mix. These mixes provide extra drainage for containers. If you can find one specifically for vegetable containers, that is even better.

As you continually water your containers, over time the mix will compact and remove the air pockets that roots need. Therefore, it is best to change your soil mix completely every few years. In between and to stretch it further, you may add fresh compost and fertilizer every year.

CONTAINER MIX INGREDIENTS

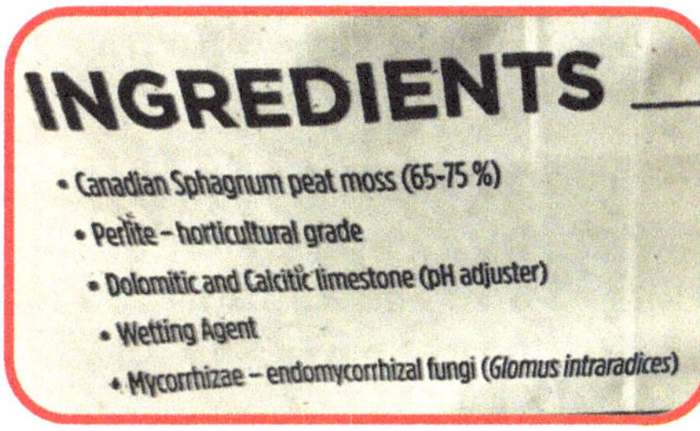

Below are the typical ingredients you will find in a container mix.

- ***Peat moss (or coir).*** Peat moss is not a sustainable product and can deplete aged bogs. Therefore, the horticulture industry is moving towards coir, which is made from coconut husks. Both peat and coir hold moisture, but coir tends to hold more.
- ***Compost.*** Compost is organic matter used to amend soil. It is a myth that the primary purpose of compost is to provide nutrients, although it will provide some, depending upon the type. In reality, compost improves the ability to retain nutrients, as well as water. It is also known for its ability to improve soil structure, providing beneficial air pockets for roots, which get eliminated over time with watering. The air pockets also give young roots something to more easily expand into. This is especially important with root crops, which need loose soil to develop. And compost helps moderate soil pH. All this increases plant vigor and resistance to pests and diseases. There are many types of compost, typically broken down into these categories:
    - ***Manures.*** These contain mostly nitrogen with some micronutrients.
    - ***Leaf litter/mushroom.*** These have beneficial microbes and bacteria.

  - ***Earthworm castings.*** These also have beneficial microbes and bacteria. If your mix does not have compost in it, you can add it on your own. Most people buy compost in bags, but you can also make your own, a process that uses bins (there are many different types), takes time to process, effort to turn, and needs the appropriate amount of materials, heat, and water.

- ***Perlite and/or coarse sand.*** Perlite is the little white pieces you see in mixes. It is a volcanic product that is heated until it puffs up. It provides excellent drainage. Sand will also provide drainage. However, be sure to use coarse sand and not play sand, which can condense to a cement-like texture. Vermiculite is sometimes used for drainage, but it also retains water.

- ***Mycorrhizae fungi.*** This is a beneficial fungus that attaches to the roots of plants to form a symbiotic relationship. It allows more nutrients to be absorbed by the plant and helps plants better tolerate stress, such as transplanting and diseases.
- ***Wetting agent.*** A wetting agent makes it easier for the initial wetting of the mix. Otherwise, you may have to soak the soil before it will absorb water. Although all the other ingredients above can be found in organic form, a wetting agent usually prevents a mix from being organic. Although I prefer organic mixes, I usually try to find one with a wetting agent because it is much easier and saves time.
- ***Fertilizer.*** Some mixes come with fertilizer already added, but many times the fertilizer may not be organic. You can add your own instead when filling your container. (I prefer to add my own since I am particular about using organic products and good-quality fertilizers.)

There are also "complete" mix products that come with moisture control. The moisture control granules look like rock salt pieces at first. As they absorb water, they expand to look like mini jellyfish. They then release that water slowly back into the soil. If your containers are outside and you are growing in our rainy season, be sure your container has a drainage hole so the mix does not become waterlogged. These products are not organic.

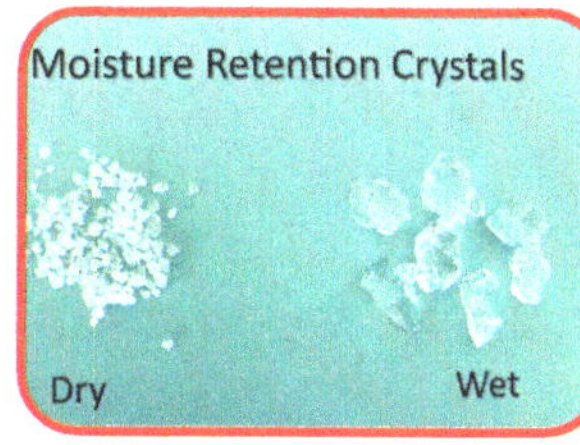

STAKES

Most tall vegetable plants will need to be staked for support. Typically, this includes vining types such as tomatoes, cucumbers, squash, and sometimes larger pepper plants. If the fruit becomes too heavy, you can place a mesh bag around it and tie it to the stake. Corn stalks, although very tall, are strong enough on their own and do not need staking.

Stakes can be used in the garden or in containers. Add stakes before planting; otherwise, you could disturb or accidentally rip the roots of your plants if you add them later. If you must do it later, do it very gingerly.

There are many types of stakes. Stronger ones, like trellises, can be used for vegetable plants with heavier fruit, such as squash and cucumbers. Tomatoes can use tomato cages, good for their multi-branching pattern. There are several shapes and sizes. Some vining tomatoes will still outgrow these cages (see more in Part 2 Tomatoes).

Cukes on trellis stake

Curly stakes are cool-looking and come in different colors to make a beautiful presentation in the garden. However, they are best for smaller plants that still need some support and have single stems such as peppers or smaller tomatoes. There are also simple stick-like wood or plastic stakes, typically in red, green, or natural.

Wooden/plastic stakes

Curly stakes on peppers

Curly stakes

Depending upon the type of stake, you may need to tie the plant branches to it, and there are many types of ties as well—string, stretchy plastic, twist-ties, Velcro, etc. Any will work just fine, but I find Velcro easiest to use, and I am able to reuse it every season. Just be sure to tie somewhat loosely so that it does not cut off the circulation of the stem as it continues to grow. Also, a little leeway allows the stems to flex in the wind, which prevents breakage and makes them stronger.

TRANSPLANTING

I like to do a final watering 2-3 days before transplanting. This leaves the mix with the perfect amount of moisture so that it does not fall off the roots as you remove the plant. Transplant on a cloudy day or late in the day; otherwise your baby plants may melt in the heat.

If transplanting from a cell pack, use a small seedling spade, a butter knife, or the end of a spoon to gently lift out the plant.

If using grower pots, turn the pot sideways and gently pull out the plant. If it does not readily come out, you can gently squeeze the sides once all around. Be sure to take the entire root system and its soil, trying to keep everything together. After removing the plant, if you see that it is root-bound (roots are very tightly entangled), gently tease the roots apart. If using peat pots or soil blocks, do not remove the plants since they will be placed directly in the ground.

Some plants have a harder time with transplanting. I personally have not had issues, but just be extra careful with these plants (cucumber, squash, etc.). If you do have problems, try peat pellets or peat pots next time.

Plant so that the pot's soil is at the same level as the soil in your container or garden. If using peat pots, bury the entire pot in the soil, or rip off the top portion above the soil line. If part of the peat pot is showing, it will wick moisture away from the plant, and the plant will not thrive. After planting, water in your new garden/container.

PLANT CARE

Once you have planted, it is time to properly care for your plants to achieve a successful harvest. General tips are below. But care needs vary by crop, and the specifics are noted in Part 2 of this book.

LIGHT

Most vegetables need full sun, which is considered 6 hours per day. But some vegetables can take partial shade. If you are growing indoors, you can use grow lights (see details in the previous Seeding section).

WATERING

Water needs vary. Some vegetable plants are shallow-rooted and, as a result, will need more water on a regular basis. Young vegetable plants will not need as much initially, but as they continue to grow, they will need more. Containers use more water than outdoor gardens, which hold onto water better. If your container or garden has a lot of compost (versus sand), it will retain water better. And vegetable plants in full sun will need more than shade crop plants.

Generally, new plants need 1 inch of water per week, and 1-2 inches for established plants. If growing in a container (or even a garden), you can test using a water meter. Push the tip down to where the tiny feeder roots are (about 2 inches) to get an accurate reading because it is okay for the top to be slightly dry. For containers, water slowly and thoroughly until water runs out the bottom.

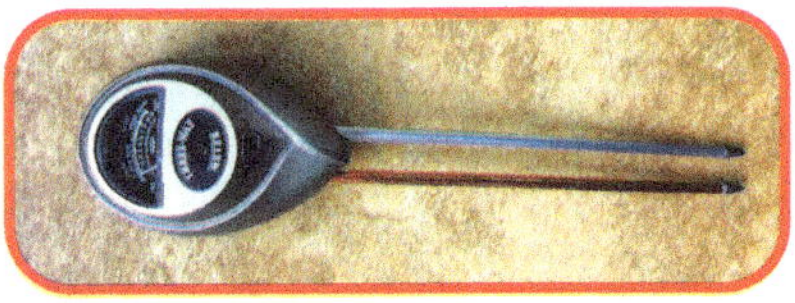

For in-ground gardens, the easiest way to water is via soaker hoses or drip irrigation. In other parts of the country, it is easy to attach the hoses to a timer to make everything automatic. You can do that in Florida also, but beware that, with our tropical environment, you will have to adjust the timer based on whether we are in the dry season or rainy season. A better option is to invest in a unit with a rain gauge.

Be sure to water the soil and not the foliage, which can encourage fungal diseases.

WATER QUALITY

You should understand the quality of the water you are using on your vegetables to ensure they are safe to eat. In my community, water from our outdoor faucets is potable, meaning it is safe to drink. But our irrigation water is reclaimed, meaning it is stormwater runoff collected in water retention areas or groundwater from the lower Floridan aquifer when supplies are not available.

Therefore, my community's recommendation is that if you are watering using a hose from your outdoor faucet, your vegetables are fine. But if your garden or containers are being watered via irrigation, vegetables should be cooked first before eating.

FERTILIZING

Vegetable plants use up nutrients throughout the growing season, and fertilizer needs vary by crop and other factors. Gardens and containers with plenty of compost will not need as much fertilizer because compost helps retain nutrients. Containers will need more fertilizer than in-ground gardens since nutrients wash out faster. Some crops are heavy feeders whereas others are moderate. And some do not need much at all since they are soil-fixers and make their own (legumes).

FERTILIZER COMPONENTS

Fertilizers include major nutrients called macronutrients, also known as N-P-K.

- ***N = Nitrogen.*** Nitrogen helps plant foliage. Leafy vegetables, such as lettuce, therefore need plenty of nitrogen.
- ***P = Phosphorus.*** Phosphorus is for plants that produce flowers. Fruiting vegetables, such as tomatoes, peppers, and cucumbers, therefore need phosphorus. If growing an in-ground garden, Florida soils already have plenty of phosphorus naturally and you may not need more. Too much phosphorus is a leading cause of our lakes getting polluted.
- ***K = Potassium.*** Potassium is needed for root health, overall plant health, and disease prevention. This is needed for all types of vegetables, but especially for root crops such as carrots and potatoes.

Fertilizers vary in how much of each of those major nutrients they contain. For instance, a fertilizer listed as 10-10-10 is considered a balanced fertilizer and has equal proportions of all the major nutrients. This is generally what is used in containers, and in gardens that do not already have enough phosphorus naturally.

Fertilizers may also contain micronutrients, such as calcium and magnesium, as well as other ingredients such as vitamins, probiotics, and mycorrhizal fungi.

TYPES OF FERTILIZERS

Fertilizers come in two types. A water-soluble liquid fertilizer, usually diluted to half strength, can be used every few weeks.

The other option is granular slow-release fertilizer, which requires less maintenance and is typically used for vegetable crops. Due to our environmental conditions, these fertilizers break down quicker in Central Florida than elsewhere north of Florida. Sometimes, the granules may not break down at all if temperatures are too hot. Generally, a slow-release product is applied 2-3 times during the growing season.

If you are growing leafy vegetables, I would recommend liquid fish emulsion. For fruiting vegetables, I would recommend getting a slow-release fertilizer specifically meant for vegetable crops. If you are growing tomatoes, you can even find one specifically for those. Organic products will have the OMRI or other organic designation right on the label. There are many organic brands on the market to choose from, which I would recommend for anything you plan on eating!

You can also use kelp (seaweed), an organic product that adds micronutrients and growth hormones and increases flower production. It can be applied as a soil drench, or as a spray for foliage, especially when a plant starts blooming.

FERTILIZER FOLKLORE

Ever hear this one? "My grandfather used banana peels in the planting hole, and his vegetables came out great!" Well, yes, there is some truth to those tales, but use some caution when it comes to vegetable plants.

- ***Coffee grounds.*** Contain nitrogen and organic matter; can assist with disease suppression. However, some plants (nightshade family of tomatoes, peppers, and more) can be sensitive to caffeine.
- ***Animal manures.*** Rabbit, chicken, etc. Contain nitrogen.

- ***Wood ash.*** Contains potassium. But can also raise pH.
- ***Banana peels.*** Contain potassium.

The main drawback with these solutions is that they usually provide a single nutrient. And in general, unless you know you have a particular soil problem, balanced solutions work best.

PRUNING AND HILLING

Some plants will need additional care as they grow. (See specifics for applicable crops in the next part of this book.)

Tomatoes, depending on type, may need to be pruned to remove suckers.

Some crops, such as cucumbers and beans, need to be continually harvested for the plant to keep producing. Otherwise, the plant will think it has done its job creating seeds for reproduction and will cease putting out fruit.

Some root crops will need to be "hilled," such as potatoes and leeks. This involves hilling up additional soil around the vegetable as it grows, thereby keeping it underground and tender.

PESTS AND DISEASES

PESTS

Pests can be a larger problem in Central Florida because our winters are not cold enough to knock down their numbers. If growing outside, you will have problems with larger insects and pests. If you are growing under screening, like in a lanai or birdcage, you will have more problems with smaller pests because they are able to get through the screening, yet the larger insects cannot do so.

Some of the small soft-bodied insects that are commonly found on many vegetables are listed below. Pests that are usually specific to a given crop are listed in Section 2 for that crop.

- ***Aphids.*** These are green or dark-colored tiny insects that usually hang out on the underside of leaves. The leaves have a speckled look and may curl or turn brown. Aphids excrete a sticky honeydew substance that can attract a black fungus called sooty mold. Ants love honeydew, so if you see them, check for aphids.
- ***Whiteflies.*** Just as the name says, these are tiny white flies that are somewhat easy to see on leaves or, when you shake the plant, will fly. They will spread viruses.
- ***Mites.*** Too tiny to see without a powerful hand lens, but you can tap the plant over a sheet of white paper and they will fall onto it. Sometimes you can see their webbing. But most often, you will know it is mites by the result of their feeding leaving a stippled mottling on the leaves.
- ***Thrips.*** You will have to look very closely to see these insects, which look like a tiny sliver. They are usually found on succulent new growth. Their feeding may result in speckled silvery patches on the leaves, and the leaves may curl. They spread viruses.

- ***Leaf Miners.*** These are fly larvae that eat through the interior of a leaf, leaving their trails behind. By the time you see the trails, they most likely have moved on. It is hard to find a systemic chemical that can be used safely on edible crops. The trails do not look good, but they do not harm the fruit, and you can merely cut off the affected leaves if they bother you. Leaf miners are very common on tomato plants.

Some other pests are listed below.

- ***Lubbers.*** These are huge grasshoppers and they love to eat. They leave large holes in leaves. If you can find them when young, you have a better chance of controlling them.
- ***Nematodes.*** These microscopic worms are found in the soil, but you may see their damage via wilting plants. They are hard to get rid of. You can solarize your soil by covering the ground with plastic and letting the sun bake it for 6-8 weeks in the heat of summer. Growing in containers will prevent this.
- ***Caterpillars.*** These include army worms, cut worms, loopers, and more. They leave ragged holes in the tops of leaves. Use Bt, an organic product, to kill.
- ***Slugs/snails.*** They like to come out at night, but you can usually see their silvery trails in the daylight. They also leave ragged holes in leaves, starting from the base of the plant and working their way up. There are many organic granular products or fun methods (salt melts them) to try on your own.
- ***Rabbits.*** Fencing or chicken wire works best for all smaller animals. Be sure to dig it down one foot so they cannot get underneath. Unfortunately, fencing is not allowed in some communities, but if you use a black wire one, it usually cannot be seen from afar. You can also try growing garlic or use garlic clips on your garden perimeter.

There are repellents, including natural red pepper, but they need to be reapplied constantly after rains. Plastic snakes, surprisingly, seem to be very effective, perhaps because rabbits have bad eyesight. And if you find a real snake skin, leave it!

CONTROLLING PESTS

Follow IPM – integrated pest management – for best results while balancing a healthy environment. It means starting with the least toxic approach first, then moving up to more caustic chemicals as needed. Regularly perform monitoring, which you can do by sight or by using sticky traps. Make sure you identify the pest properly before spraying, so you do not accidentally kill a good insect instead of a bad one.

Insecticidal soap is relatively safe and kills smaller soft-bodied insects on contact. It is helpful for aphids, whiteflies, spider mites, and thrips. Neem oil, which is organic, or its synthetic equivalent called Horticultural oil, kills by smothering pests such as mealy bugs. Bt, an organic beneficial microbial product, can be used for caterpillars and worms. Spinosad, another organic product made from naturally occurring microbial bacteria in soils, is effective at killing many different pests. Make sure to spray underneath the leaves also, where pests like to hide. And keep spraying for several weeks throughout the insect's life cycle.

Another way to control pests is via beneficial insects. Lacewings and ladybugs are two of the most common and are typically mail-ordered. Water your vegetables first, then release them. Normally, they will stick around for only a short period of time and then fly away.

DISEASES

There are many diseases that impact vegetable plants. Some even affect the soil so that you cannot grow there again. When I lived in New England, I had a tomato fail in a particular location. I tried for several years and just could not grow another tomato in that same spot. I eventually planted a different vegetable there successfully.

Diseases fall into three categories: fungal, bacterial, and viral. Accurate diagnosing can be difficult without lab tests or a high-powered microscope.

- ***Fungal.*** Symptoms include spots on leaves, frequently with yellow halos known as rust. Fungus comes from soil, particularly when wet. To prevent, cut foliage up from the base of the plant to prevent fungus from splashing up (see Section 2 Tomatoes for more information). Make sure you are not watering from overhead. Use a fungicide product safe for vegetables.
- ***Bacterial.*** Blights are when leaves turn yellow and the plant just dies. Wilts are when the plant dies without yellow leaves, but if you cut open the stem, it will be brown inside. Blights happen more in wet weather. The solution for these bacterial problems is to destroy the plant. And because the bacteria is in the soil, try to plant a different crop from a different vegetable family in that spot next year.
- ***Viral.*** Viral issues are often confused with fertilizer deficiencies. The difference is that viral problems have a non-uniform pattern on the leaves, whereas nutrient problems are symmetrical. Similar to bacterial issues, the solution is to destroy the plant and plant a different crop family in that spot next year.

The best strategy is to know which diseases affect which crops and use hybrid seeds that have been bred to handle those diseases. For example, see the Tomato section in Part 2 for a list of the many diseases and some of the tomato varieties that are resistant to them. Be sure to do a good cleanup of your garden at year's end.

HARVESTING

Harvesting of cool-weather crops can happen throughout the winter months but is usually over by March when our Central Florida temperatures start climbing. For warm-weather crops grown in spring, harvest is over by early June, when we enter our really hot weather. Harvesting of warm-season vegetables grown in fall usually happens by early December, when temperatures start to dip.

Many vegetables are eaten fresh. Some last longer, such as potatoes. And some, such as winter squashes, can be stored in a cool, dry place (do you have a root cellar?) for months.

Some vegetables need to be cured before storing. This allows the skin of root vegetables to dry and harden, which protects the crop from rot before moving indoors for storage.

Butternut squash curing in my garden

Another fun method of storage is canning, such as with tomatoes. Proper technique (beyond the scope of this book) must be followed to prevent botulism. Cucumbers can be pickled, something my grandmother showed me how to do as a child.

As you are growing, keep track of your successes and failures. It is a great learning tool and will help you remember for next year when it is time to buy seeds again.

After you harvest, particularly for crops that you grew different varieties of, such as tomatoes, do a taste test! Invite your family and friends if you would like, they will be happy to participate. Note which ones are winners that you would like to re-grow next year.

HYDROPONICS

SEEDING

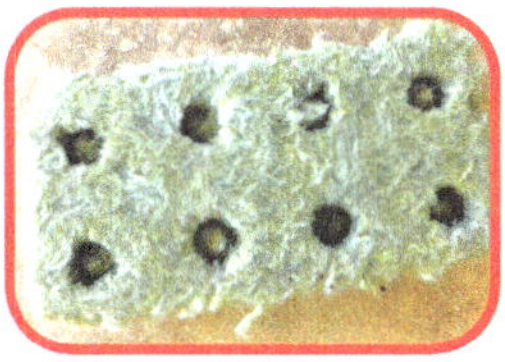

You can find seeds that specifically indicate they are meant for hydroponic purposes, but this is not a requirement. They are normally for smaller-growing vegetable plants, such as dwarf tomatoes and lettuce.

For hydroponic growing, seeding usually starts outside the hydroponic unit. Rock wool is the standard medium used, and it comes with pre-formed holes.

Place each rock wool square in a cell, cup with a hole punched in the bottom, or directly in a tray. Add water and let soak for a few hours until the squares are moist. Then seed as usual.

Once the seedlings have obtained their second set of true leaves, transplant them into your hydroponic unit.

Hydroponic pots with clay pebbles

GROWING

You will need to fertilize regularly with a liquid fertilizer, usually done each time you need to add water to the unit. Be sure to buy the correct nutrient solution for the type of plant you are growing. Greens, such as lettuce, need mostly nitrogen, whereas fruiting vegetables will need something with phosphorus to enhance flowering.

Be sure to monitor the pH in these systems (usually via test strips). Same as with regular growing—if your pH is incorrect, it will prevent the uptake of nutrients.

Be sure to maintain your water levels. And eventually you may need to refresh entirely with clean water.

PART 2 – SPECIFIC VEGETABLES

HOW TO USE PART 2

Here in Part 2, vegetables are categorized in sections by their growing season for Central Florida – hot, cool, or warm, plus indoor microgreens. Within each seasonal section, important points for each vegetable are noted. At the end of each section is a quick reference chart that has detailed information on each individual vegetable – characteristics, seeding/germination/transplanting, growing, plant care, and harvesting.

Most vegetables can be grown in containers, although some will need to be trellised, and larger ones may not get more than one plant in a single container. However, not all can be grown in lanais.

SUMMER/HOT VEGETABLES

GROWING IN SUMMER

It can be difficult to grow vegetables in the Central Florida heat of summer. Some that do well include Malabar spinach (not a true spinach), okra, sweet potatoes, and southern/black-eyed peas. Some cool and warm season crops can extend into the summer, such as collards, peppers, and cherry tomatoes, including the variety called 'Everglades.'

MALABAR SPINACH

Malabar spinach is not a true spinach. It tastes similar but with a milder citrus-like flavor. It is a vining plant with either green or red stems. The best part is that it provides summer greens when little else grows.

OKRA

Okra is a true southern plant that loves the sun. The pods, which come in either green, red, or white, are the edible part. The flowers, pale yellow with maroon centers, are pretty.

Red okra growing in my friend Anne's garden (right photo)

SWEET POTATOES

Sweet potato plants grow as vines. The potatoes can be dug up and harvested at any time by digging up the tubers, but they are done growing when the leaves turn yellow. Cure in the sun or a warm area with humidity for up to 2 weeks. Greens can also be eaten. If your potatoes are cracked, it means you have nematodes. Grow in a different location next year, or use containers.

QUICK REFERENCE CHART

HOT SEASON VEGETABLES				
Vegetable	Design		Seeding & Transplanting	Trans. Diff.
	Family	Poll.		
Malabar Spinach	Basella	None	• Green and red stemmed varieties , with vining habit. • Slow germination, soak seeds for 24 hours.	M
Okra	Hibiscus	Self	• Colors include green, red, white. • Soak seeds before planting.	H
Sweet Potato	Morning glory	None	• Grown from rooted cuttings called slips. Make your own by letting an organic sweet potato sprout, then when 6 inches long, twist off the sprouts. Place in water or mix until roots form. • Use compact varieties.	L

QUICK REFERENCE CHART

HOT SEASON VEGETABLES					
Growing	Plant Care				Harvesting
	Light	Water	Nutrients	Pests/Diseases	
• Vining habit, needs a trellis. • Red stem variety may act as a perennial.	S-PS	Moderate (not enough = bitter)	Moderate		• Harvest leaves once plant is full size. • Flavor is mild and citrus-like.
• Large plants need room. • Pretty yellow flowers with dark red centers. • Stems, leaves, pods have tiny spines, wear gloves.	S	Consistent, Heavy	Moderate	- Nematodes	• Keep picking or crop will cease. • Harvest pods at 2-3 inches and shortly after flowers have fallen. Otherwise, tough fruit.
• Grows as a vine along the ground. • Need a long growing season. • If growing in-ground, rotate to a new area every 3 years.	S	Moderate, consistent	Moderate, but low nitrogen	- Sweet potato weevil - Nematodes (cracked tubers)	Harvested at any time by digging up tubers, but they are done growing when leaves turn yellow. • Cure in sun or warm area with humidity for up to 2 weeks. • Greens can also be eaten.

COOL SEASON VEGETABLES

GROWING IN THE COOL MONTHS

Many cool-weather crops are good for succession planting, repeatedly replanted throughout the season for a continual crop.

BEETS

Beets come in different colors—red, purple, and golden—and cooler temperatures bring out the best color. Make sure to give seeds adequate moisture to germinate. Each "seed" actually contains multiple seeds, so you will need to thin out. Beets are good for containers and succession planting.

As they are growing, hill up the soil so they remain underground and more tender. Keep the soil/mix moist to prevent cracking. Harvest when approximately 2 inches in diameter. The young greens can also be eaten.

BROCCOLI

Broccoli is grown for its immature flowers. It has a long growing season, so plant in the fall (warm weather will cause it to bolt). Use mini varieties for containers.

To harvest, use a knife to cut the broccoli head on the main stem when the flower buds are dark green and unopened (yellow means they are starting to open). The side shoots will continue to produce more florets, as long as you continually harvest them.

CABBAGE

There are several kinds of cabbages:

- ***Regular***
- ***Savoy*** - which has wrinkled leaves
- ***Chinese*** - which can be either open-leaf (like Bok Choy) or have a head. Chinese varieties are quicker to grow.

Heading varieties can be grown in containers, but try to use compact varieties. Cabbage has shallow roots and needs even moisture. Otherwise, heads will split. It does best with heavy fertilizer.

Although they are generally easy to grow, cabbages are challenged by pests such as cabbage worm and looper, which leave holes in the leaves. However, they can be controlled with regular monitoring and Bt.

CARROTS

Carrots are so colorful – they come in orange, purple, white, and yellow. And orange was not the original color! Some say white was, and orange was bred as a cross between purple and yellow, and purposely made sweeter.

Many sizes are available, from mini varieties (good for containers) to longer ones. The key to carrots is making sure they have a light soil/mix to produce length.

Carrot seeds are very tiny, so cover them lightly. They are very slow to germinate. And you will have to thin them out, so each carrot has enough width to grow.

Make sure they have enough moisture, especially during germination. It should be even moisture; too much during the growing season will result in cracking. Fertilize, but do not overdo the nitrogen because it causes tough skin and cracking.

Harvest when fully colored, and not too late, or they will become woody. If nematodes are an issue, grow in containers.

CELERY

Celery is grown for its stalks. Related crops are celeriac, grown for its bulb, and celery leaf, an herb (one of my favorites – refer to my Growing Fresh Herbs book for more information). Celery has a long growing season, so it can sometimes be difficult to grow in Central Florida.

Celery seeds can be tough to germinate—they need light, warmth, and moisture. To save time, you can start with store-bought celery, remove the stalks 2-3 inches from the base (above the white part), then plant in soil or mix.

Celery has shallow roots, so be sure to provide adequate moisture. If not enough, stalks become tough and lose flavor. Provide heavy fertilization. Harvest individual stalks from the outside, or cut the entire plant at the base. Water the day before for best flavor and optimal storage length.

COLLARD GREENS

Related to cabbage, collard greens are known as a southern staple, grown for their leafy greens. Although collards can be grown in summer also, their leaves are sweeter and taste better in cool weather. If growing in containers, they will need a tall and deep pot. Harvest lower leaves first, and before they turn bitter.

GARLIC

There are several types of garlic:

- ***Hardneck*** -These need cold, and are therefore not grown in Florida. They produce scapes that are also eaten.
- ***Softneck*** -This is the best variety for Florida. The soft neck can be used for braiding.
- ***Elephant garlic*** - These are bigger bulbs and cloves, and they have a milder taste. They are particularly grown in California.

Garlic "seeds" are cloves, separated from the bulb, and found in farm stores or online. Or, you can save a bulb from your prior year's crop. Use the largest cloves, which will create the largest plants/bulbs. If your garlic does not produce fully formed big bulbs, next year try placing the bulbs in your refrigerator for approximately 3 months prior to planting, a process called vernalization. Mulching, even in containers, will help provide a cooler root environment. Plant in fall, with the pointy end of the clove upwards.

Harvest in spring when half of the leaves have dried and fallen over (usually the bottom ones). Cure after harvest by laying in the sun for 2 weeks, then trim stems and roots. (Cover or bring inside if it rains.)

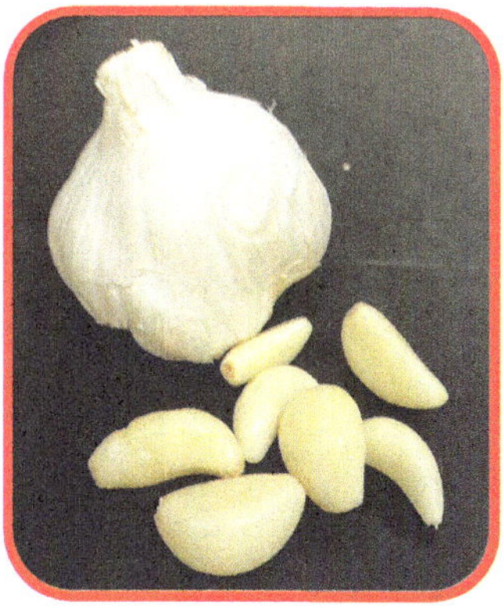

KALE

There are several types of kale:

- ***Lacinato*** (wrinkly)
- ***Siberian/Russian*** (smooth leaves)
- ***Curly***

Note: Ornamental varieties exist and are not grown to eat.

For container gardening, use compact varieties. Ensure consistent moisture, or else the leaves become tough. Fish emulsion works well as a fertilizer. Cold weather increases its sweet flavor. When harvesting, pick leaves from the bottom up.

LEEKS

Leeks are similar to onions, but they are larger, milder, and sweeter. The main thing about growing leeks is to hill soil/mix around the plant base as it grows to obtain longer blanched (white) stems, which is the edible plant part. If growing in a container, leave 6" on top for hilling, and add more soil as growth occurs.

Leeks need heavy fertilization, especially nitrogen, and fish emulsion or seaweed work well. When harvesting, pull out the entire plant. For cooking, use the white stem base.

LETTUCE

Red romaine growing in my hydroponic garden

There are different types of lettuce:

- ***Leaf/Looseleaf*** - Does best for FL.
- ***Romaine/Cos*** - Tolerates warmer weather.
- ***Butterhead/Bibb***
- ***Crisphead/Iceberg*** - As its name implies, it is harder to grow in Florida.
- ***Mesclun*** - Mix of romaine, leaf, and others.

Lettuce comes in different colors from green to red. Lettuce is one of the easiest crops to grow and is great for hydroponics and containers. Because it is a fast grower, succession planting every two weeks for a continuous crop is recommended.

Lettuce seeds need cool temps to germinate (do not use a heating mat). They also need light to germinate, so sow on top of the soil/mix or cover very lightly.

The key to the tastiest lettuce is rapid growth. Continually fertilize with fish emulsion. Water regularly since lettuce is shallow-rooted. Mulch will help, even in containers.

Harvest individual outer leaves (unless lettuce is the type to form a head), use the cut-and-come-again method of cutting two inches above the base (which will regrow for another crop), or harvest the entire plant.

Red romaine growing in my hydroponic garden

Below are some of the lettuces I have grown here in Florida on my lanai or hydroponically. They tend to be more compact varieties. I particularly like the pretty red lettuce varieties.

LETTUCE		
Description	**Type**	**Color**
Buttercrunch (organic) Full sized. Forms a small, open but tightly bunched, 6" rosette that is fan-shaped rather than round. Dark green leaves. Crisp and sweet. Slow bolting.	Bibb	Green
Rex (organic,pellet) Slow to bolt. Resistant to downy mildew. The standard for hydroponics. Not recommended for outdoors.	Butterhead	Green
Alkindus (organic) Dense mini heads with shiny red somewhat savoy-textured leaves. Resistant to downy mildew and lettuce mosaic virus. Can be used for hydroponics also.	Butterhead	Red
Breen (organic) Compact, 8" tall. Mini head or leaf lettuce. Medium bronze red. Can be used for hydroponics also.	Romaine	Red
Dragoon (organic) Mini, compact. Leaves are thick and have an excellent, crisp texture. Heads are very dense. Bolting and tipburn tolerant. Suitable for hydroponic systems. Resistant downy mildew and lettuce mosaic virus. Can be used for hydroponics also.	Romaine	Green
Truchas (organic) Compact mini heads, 6-8" tall. Resistant to downy mildew and lettuce mosaic virus. Can be used for hydroponics also.	Romaine	Red
Salanova Red Butter (organic,pellet) Dense rosette heads with round base and attractive, thin, supple open leaves. Red to green color transition. Delicate, buttery flavor. Resistance to downy mildew. Very good bolt tolerance. Excellent for hydroponics.	Romaine	Red

ONIONS

There are three types of onions:

- ***Short-day.*** Best for Florida.
- ***Long-day.*** Best for northern parts of the country.
- ***Day-neutral.*** Can be grown anywhere.

Onions come in various colors - white (mild), yellow (sweet), and red. You may have heard about Vidalia onions – they are a sweet variety grown only in Vidalia, Georgia, which claims the soil there makes them extra sweet. There are other onion-like crops, including shallots, which have a delicate flavor, scallions (or green/bunching), and leeks.

Seeds are actually "sets" (mini bulbs). Plant in the fall with the tips up. Ensure evenly moist soil/mix, since onions can split if too dry. Harvest in spring when tops fall over. Cure after harvest by laying out in the sun for 1 week, then trim stems and roots.

Red, white,
sweet Vadalia

PEAS

When thinking of peas, we usually think of the English kind, which includes several types:

- ***Shell*** (must be shelled from pods)
- ***Snap*** (can eat pods and peas inside)
- ***Snow*** (pods before peas develop)

But there is also the Southern kind, a snap type, known as black-eyed peas, which, unlike English varieties, can be grown in summer.

Peas grow as bush types and vine types, with the latter needing a trellis. Peas are a soil-fixing crop, and will not need as much nitrogen. You will need to harvest continually to keep them producing.

Snap Peas.

POTATOES

Regular potatoes, known as Irish potatoes, are a cool-season crop. Sweet potatoes are different and grow in the summer. (They can be found under the Hot Weather Crops section.)

Potatoes come in various colors – white, gold, red, and blue. Each "seed" is a tuber piece containing two eyes, and will produce 6-8 potatoes. You can create your own, but be sure to select an organic potato, since regular grocery store potatoes have been treated to prevent sprouting. After cutting them into pieces, let them dry for several days before planting.

Plant in late winter. As they grow, hill up the soil around the base of the plants. It will create more tubers and also prevent sunlight exposure, which results in green potatoes and a toxin. "Grow bags" or containers are great for potatoes, just leave the top 6" open for hilling. Provide plenty of fertilizer.

Harvest at any size, but growth will stop after plant leaves turn yellow in spring. Cure potatoes for 2 weeks in the shade.

RADISHES

There are two types of radishes – summer and winter (the latter also known as Oriental, including the Daikon radish variety). They come in various colors such as red, white, and purple.

Radishes are small vegetables, great for containers. They are also fast-growing, which is good for succession planting every two weeks. Be sure they get adequate moisture, otherwise they turn bitter. They are prone to pests such as aphids and flea beetles.

Harvest at approximately 1½ inches in diameter, before they become tough and bitter. The greens can also be eaten when young (if older, they become bitter).

SCALLIONS

Scallions are also known as green or bunching onions. Unlike regular onions, they do not form a bulb and are eaten for their flavorful stems. They are one of the few perennial vegetables, meaning they will continue to come back year after year, even after a freeze.

The seeds are hard and take longer to germinate. I have had good success by soaking them for 24 hours before seeding. I have also had good success by starting with grocery store scallions. I cut off the top growth 2 inches above the base for use in cooking, then place the ends in water until the tops start growing again (they may be somewhat dry after their grocery store journey). I ultimately place them in soil/mix. I also have good success growing them hydroponically.

SPINACH

There are different types of spinach, including smooth and savoy (the latter having wrinkled leaves). There is also a vegetable called Malabar spinach, which is not a true spinach and grows in the summer months (see Hot Weather Crops section).

Spinach seeds need cool temperatures to germinate. It is a good crop for succession planting every 2 weeks. The soil/mix should have a pH of 6.5-7.5, which is slightly more alkaline. Give consistent water and fertilizer, but too much nitrogen can make the leaves turn bitter.

Harvest individual outer leaves or the entire plant. "Baby spinach" is young spinach, and more tender.

QUICK REFERENCE CHART

COOL SEASON VEGETABLES				
Vegetable	**Design**		**Seeding & Transplanting**	**Trans. Diff.**
	Family	**Poll.**		
Beet	Beet	None	• Different colors - red, purple, golden. • Seeds need adequate moisture to germinate. • Each "seed" actually contains multiple seeds, so thin out. • Good for succession planting, every 2 weeks.	L
Broccoli	Cabbage	None	• For containers, use mini varieties.	L
Cabbage - Regular - Savoy -wrinkled leaves - Chinese - open leaf like Bok Choy or heading	Cabbage	None	• Green or red/purple varieties. • For containers, use compact varieties.	L
Carrot	Carrot	None	• Many sizes available from mini varieties (containers) to longer ones. • Seeds are very tiny, cover lightly. • Slow to germinate. • Thin out for enough room. • Good for succession sowing.	M

QUICK REFERENCE CHART

COOL SEASON VEGETABLES					
Growing	Plant Care				Harvesting
	Light	Water	Nutrients	Pests/Diseases	
• Fairly fast growing. • Cool termperatures result in the best color. • Hill up soil over beets as they grow, for more tenderness.	S-PS	Consistent (otherwise beets crack, become tough and bitter). Mulch will help.	Moderate	- Leaf miners - Flea beetles	• Harvest at 2" diameter on average (see seed packet), usually when the tops are 6 inches tall. • Young greens can also be eaten.
• May not survive a freeze, and may bolt as warm weather approaches.	S-PS	Consistent	Heavy nitrogen	- Cabbage worm - Flea beetles	• Using a knife, cut the broccoli head on the main stem when the flower bugs are dark green and unopened (yellow means they are starting to open). • Side shoots will continue to produce more florets, as long as you continually harvest them.
• Chinese varieties grow quicker.	S	Consistent (shallow roots, uneven=split heads)	Heavy (keep fertilizing)	- Cabbage worm,loopers - Slugs - Flea beetles	• Harvest leaves or when heads are full and firm. • Some varieties store longer than others.
• Need loose soil to produce length.	S-PS	Moderate (too much = cracking)	Moderate (too much N causes forking and tough skin)	- Nematodes	• Harvest when full colored. • If too mature, will get woody.

QUICK REFERENCE CHART

COOL SEASON VEGETABLES				
Vegetable	Design		Seeding & Transplanting	Trans. Diff.
	Family	Poll.		
Celery	Carrot	None	• Needs light to germinate. • Slow to germinate, needs warmth and plenty of moisture. To save time, start with store-bought celery, remove the starts 3 minches from the based (above the white part), then plant in soil.	M
Collard Greens	Caggage	None	• May be grown summer also, but leaves are sweeter and taste better in cool weather.	?
Garlic - Hardneck (not for FL) - Softneck (FL) - Elephant	Onion	None	• "Seeds" are cloves, separated from bulb. • Make your own by saving a bulb from prior year's crop. Use the larges cloves for the largest plants/bulbs. • Place garlic in your refrigerator for approximatley 3 months prior to planting, called vernalization. Simulating cold will spur fully formed, bigger bulbs. • Plant in Fall, pointy end up.	M
Kale	Cabbage	None	• For containers, use compact varieties.	L
Leek	Onion	None	• For containers, leave 6" on top for hilling.	M

QUICK REFERENCE CHART

COOL SEASON VEGETABLES					
Growing	Plant Care				Harvesting
	Light	Water	Nutrients	Pests/Diseases	
• Cold weather during early growth can result in bolting of a seed stem inside the stalk. • May be hard to grow in FL - long time to maturity.	S-PS	Heavy (shallow roots; mulch, too little = stalks become tough and lose flavor)	Heavy; Sensitve to acid soils	- Slugs	• Water day before for best flavor and maximum storage time. • Harvest outside stalks first, or cut entire plant at the base.
• Will grow tall and need a deep pot.	S	Moderate (too much = mushy plants)	Moderate (adequate nitrogen especially)		• Harvest lower leaves first, and before they turn bitter.
• Mulch, even in containers, to provide a cooler root environment.	S-PS	Low	Moderate (too much N = more foliage, smaller bulbs)		• When half of leaves have dried and fallen over (usually the bottom ones), in spring. • Cure by laving in sun for 2 weeks, then trim stems and roots.
• Cold weather increases sweet flavor.	S	Consistent (otherwise tough leaves)	Moderate (especially needs nitrogen)	- Aphids - Slugs	• Pick leaves from the bottom up.
• Hill soil around plant base as it grows, to obtain longer blanched (white) stems - the edible part.	S	Moderate	Moderate (especially needs nitrogen)		• Pull out the entire plant. • Use the white stem base for cooking.

QUICK REFERENCE CHART

COOL SEASON VEGETABLES				
Vegetable	Design		Seeding & Transplanting	Trans. Diff.
	Family	Poll.		
Lettuce - Looseleaf - Romaine/Cos - Butterhead/Bibb - Crisphead (not FL) - Mesclun (mix of varieties)	Sunflower	None	• Great crop for hydroponics and container gardening. • Red and green varieties. • Needs cool temps (do not use heating mat) to germinate. • Needs light to germinate, sow on top of soil or cover very lightly.	L
Onion - Short-day (FL) - Long-day (not FL) - Day-neutral (anywhere)	Onion (Similar crops include leeks, shallots, scallions.)	None	• Colors include white (mild), yellow (sweet), and red. Vadalia onions are sweet onions grown only in GA. • Come as "sets" (bulbls). • Plant n Fall, pointy side up.	H
Pea English - shell, snap, snow Southern- snap	Legume	None	• Bush types and vine types (vine need trellis).	H
Potato	Nightshade	None	• Colors include white, gold, red, and blue. • Each "seed" (a tuber containing 2 eyes) will produce 6-8 potatoes. If cutting yourself, let skin dry for several days before planting. • Grocery store non-organic potatoes are sprayed to prevent sprouting. • Can be grown in containers or grow bags. Leave top 6" open for hilling.	M
Radish '- Summer - Winter/Oriental (ex. Daikon)	Cabbage	None		H

QUICK REFERENCE CHART

COOL SEASON VEGETABLES					
Growing	Plant Care				Harvesting
	Light	Water	Nutrients	Pests/Diseases	
• Rapid growth (ferrtilizer) = tastiest lettuce. • Succession plant every 2 weeks for continual crop. • Will bolt as weather warms, and leaves become bitter.	S-PS	Consistent (shallow roots; mulch)	Heavy (add plenty of compost and fertilizer)	- Slugs	• Harvest individual outer leaves (unless head-type), use cut-and-come-again method of cutting 2" above the base (which will regrow), or harvest the entire plant.
	S	Moderate (can split if too dry, mulch)	Moderate (plenty of nitrogen)		• When tops die in spring. • Cure 1 week in sun, then trim stems and roots.
• Unlike most peas, summer varieties such as Black-eye Peas, do best in warmer weather.	S	Moderate	Low (nitrogen fixing)	- Aphids	• Harvest continually to keep producing.
• Hill soil to prevent sunlight exposure (and green toxin).	S	Moderate	Heavy, use compost	- Colorado potato beetle (use Bt) - Blight	• Harvest anytime, but growth will stop after plant leaves turn yellow, in spring. • Cure for 2 weeks in shade (green = toxin).
• Fast growing. Good for succession planting every two weeks.	S	Consistent (otherwise bitter)	Low	- Aphids - Flea beetles	• Harvest at approximately 1½ inches in diameter, before they become bitter. • Greens can also be eaten, when young (older = bitter).

QUICK REFERENCE CHART

COOL SEASON VEGETABLES				
Vegetable	**Design**		**Seeding & Transplanting**	**Trans. Diff.**
	Family	**Poll.**		
Scallion (also known as bunching or green onions)	Onion	None	• Hard seeds take longer to germinate. Soak 24 hours before seeding.	H
Spinach - Smooth - Savoy - 'Malabar' (see under Hot crops)	Beet	None	• Needs cool temperatures to germinate.	M

QUICK REFERENCE CHART

COOL SEASON VEGETABLES					
Growing	Plant Care				Harvesting
	Light	Water	Nutrients	Pests/Diseases	
• These are one of the few perennial vegetables, coming back year after year.	S	Moderate	Moderate		• Harvest at any time, but cutting 2" above the base, which will then regrow.
• Ph 6.5-7.5 (towards alkaline). • "Baby spinach" is young spinach, more tender. • Good for succession crop, every two weeks.	S-PS	Consistent	Moderate (but too much nitrogen makes leaves bitter)	- Aphids	• Harvest individual outer leaves or remove entire plant.

MICROGREENS

ABOUT MICROGREENS

Microgreens are grown indoors and can, therefore, be grown year-round rather than seasonally, so they have been given their own section.

Avocado toast with microgreens, made by my vegan friend Cat

As the name implies, microgreens are green, leafy vegetables, harvested in the small seedling stage. They include lettuces, mustard greens, radish tops, carrot tops, mixed greens, and much more. In that young state, they have concentrated nutrients and powerful health benefits. Microgreens are easy and quick growing, typically taking only two weeks from seeding to harvest.

If you let them grow beyond the seedling stage, will they form a normal vegetable? Typically not - microgreen seeds are bred to be used as microgreens. For example, I let carrot microgreens grow longer than normal and they only formed a baby carrot about an inch long. But they certainly were cute!

Microgreens are sometimes confused with sprouts, which are also immature forms. However, sprouts are not grown in soil and are harvested with the seed still on before true leaves form.

SEEDING

Typically, microgreens are grown in a tray. Although you can find fancier ones available, simple restaurant takeout trays work great. Fill with seeding mix and label. Sprinkle seeds across the top. Lightly cover with more mix (unless light is needed for germination – check seed packet). Cover the tray with a dome or plastic wrap.

Place under grow lights or in a partially sunny location. Some seeds, such as carrots, take longer to germinate, but most do so within several days. Your seed packet should indicate days to germination. At that point, remove the dome.

Some systems work with jute and water. The seeds are broadcast across the top of the jute and left to germinate. It may be a bit less messy than working with a mix, but I find the greens to be a bit floppier without the support of soil. And the seeds seem to germinate sparsely.

Jute

Cabbage seedlings growing in jute

If you see an unusual white growth on jute, it is not a disease. It is the roots growing on top of the jute, and it is fine.

HARVESTING

After the first true leaves form, they are ready for harvest. Try to harvest no later than two sets of true leaves.

Kale ready to harvest

Mustard greens ready to harvest

Cut the stem slightly above the soil line, keeping the soil off the greens. Wash thoroughly before eating. They are great on salads, sandwiches, soups, smoothies, or as a garnish.

Once cut, most greens will not come back again (kale, for example, is an exception). So the process is merely started over again.

In addition to various mixes, such as mild, spicy, etc., here are some microgreens that I have successfully grown.

MICROGREENS		
Description	**Color**	**Days**
Cabbage, red Dark green, glossy leaves with purple vein and leaf margin. Mild cabbage flavor but with a touch of heat.	Red & green	10-15
Carrot Finely textured leaves with mild carrot flavor. Sprinkle over a dish to create an interesting, delicate effect.	Green	16-25
Kale Glossy, serrated red leaves with bright green stems. Mild kale flavor.	Purple & green	10-15
Mustard 'Wasabina', green Ruffled leaves with slightly spicy and sweet flavor.	Green	10-15
Mustard 'Garnet Giant', green/purple Dark purple baby leaves, with green true leaves splashed with purple and slightly toothy margins.	Purple & green	10-15
Radish, green w/red stem Fast growing with vivid deep red stems and spicy flavor.	Red & green	10-15
Scallion Green, thread-like leaves. Adds delicate pungency where a mild onion flavor is needed.	Green	16-25

WARM SEASON VEGETABLES

GROWING IN THE WARM MONTHS

Warm-weather crops, many of which are fruiting, have two seasons – spring and fall. Many people, for whatever reason, miss the fall season and only plant for spring, like we used to do when we lived in the northern part of the country. Fall here is a bonus!

For the fall season in Central Florida, plants are typically seeded indoors in July, placed outdoors (or direct-seeded) in August, and harvested by late November or December. For the spring season, plants are seeded in January indoors, placed outdoors (or direct seeded) in March, and harvested by early June.

BEANS

There are different types of beans:

- ***Pole beans***
- ***Bush beans***
- ***Snap/string***
- ***Shell***
- ***Filet beans*** (haricots verts)
- ***Lima beans***

Pole beans will need a trellis, whereas bush beans are meant more for containers. Direct sow, or be careful with transplanting (most are started directly in soil/mix). Beans are good for succession planting. Many types of beans can be eaten raw or cooked. Pole beans may taste better (sweeter, more tender) than bush.

You may see in seed catalogs that microbial inoculants increase bean yields in poor soils. However, most soils in Florida already have them naturally.

Harvest continually to keep producing. The best flavor comes from young plants. Although a warm-weather crop, beans may make it through warm Floridian winters as well.

CORN

Who doesn't love corn on the cob? But there are many kinds of sweet corn. In addition, there are other types for different purposes, such as making cornmeal, movie night popcorn, ornamental, etc.

- ***Sweet corn hybrids***
- ***Sugary*** (su)
- ***Sugar enhanced*** (se) - firm and sweet
- ***Supersweet*** (sh2) - tender and sweet
- ***Synergistic*** (syn) - combines se and sh2
- ***Field/ornamental corn*** (cornmeal, cow feed)
- ***Popcorn*** (starchy, cure first)
- ***Old-fashioned*** (open-pollinated, can be tough)

Sweet corn can be white, yellow, or bicolor. Ornamental corn is beautiful with multiple colors of blue, pink, and more. Usually, corn is direct-seeded because it can be difficult to transplant. Some kernel seeds are coated with a fungicide, which negates them from being organic and may affect good fungi in the soil.

Being so tall, plant corn on the north side of your outdoor garden, so as to not block the sun from other crops. The interesting note about corn is that it is wind pollinated. Therefore, plant in 4-row short blocks to ensure good pollination. And keep different types separate to avoid cross-pollination. This can be done by distance (planting the two crops far apart from each other), or by succession planting every 10-14 days.

Corn is shallow-rooted, so keep it consistently moist. And it is a heavy feeder, so fertilize frequently.

Corn is prone to several pests – the corn earworm (inhabits the silks) and the corn borer (infects the stems). Also, raccoons, birds, and squirrels love corn. Try tying foil ribbon, which reflects light and blows in the wind, to the plants themselves or on nearby stakes. I found that to work somewhat. You can also try fake owls, mounted on a stake in the corn patch. Scarecrows are cute, but I am not sure how well they work in my garden.

Harvest when the ends of the silks are brownish. Kernels should be milky inside (too watery are not ready). Pick in the morning for the best sweetness. And it is not a myth - eat fresh that day if possible, because the sugars turn to starch within a day after picking.

CUCUMBERS

There are several types of cucumbers:

- ***Slicing***
- ***Pickling*** (thinner skins)
- ***Burpless/seedless*** (as long as no cross-pollination)
- ***English/Japanese*** (super crisp)

Cucumbers grow in either bush form (good for containers) or vining form (need a trellis). There are two terms to know related to cucumbers. Most cucumbers are insect-pollinated, so they must be grown outdoors. However, some are parthenocarpic. The latter means they set fruit without pollination. And that means you can grow them on your lanai, in a Florida room, or in a greenhouse. And they are seedless too. Also, some varieties are gynoecious, which means they have only female flowers, and thus they produce more fruit. (However, if gynoecious, but not parthenocarpic, it will still need pollination by a regular cucumber that has male flowers.)

Transplant carefully without disturbing the roots because they can be difficult to transplant if you are not careful, or use peat pots. Cucumbers need plenty of water (otherwise, the fruit is bitter) and heavy fertilizer. They are prone to powdery mildew, a white fungal coating, or spots on leaf tops (dry, humid conditions). You can spray off the leaves, use Neem oil, or use a vegetable-safe fungicide.

Harvest small for the best taste. If too large, the fruits become bitter. Pick often to keep producing.

The cucumbers I have grown in Florida are below, meant for containers. Some are only for outdoors, but more recently, I have decided to grow solely parthenocarpic varieties, which can be placed on my lanai. Even though all of these are rated as resistant to powdery mildew, my plants still got it. The fruit was unaffected, however.

CUCUMBERS

Description	Special Characteristics	Fruit Size	Plant Ht.	Days	Disease Resist.
Diva Seedless, thin-skinned cukes are distinctly crisp, sweet, and bitter-free. AAS Winner.	Parthenocarpic Gynoecious	5-7"	60"+	58	CVYW, PM, S
Iznik Mini thin-skinned, smooth, crisp fruits. Small leaved vines, compact bush habit, good for containers.	Parthenocarpic Gynoecious	3-4"	24"	55	CMV, PM, S
Katrina Seedless, thin skinned. Sets fruit even under heat stress. Also good for hydroponics.	Parthenocarpic Gynoecious	5½–6½"	60"+	49	CMV, CVYV, PM,S
Manny Sweet with tender, shiny skins. Don't need to be supported - good for containers. Tolerates lower light. Fresh or pickled.	Parthenocarpic	5-6"	24"	50	CVYV, PM
Saladmore Bush Bushy growth habit, good for containers. Pick small for pickles. Mild, sweet flavor. Very disease resistant for South.		7-8"	24-28"	55	CMV, PM, S, Anthrac.

EGGPLANT

Most people know about purple eggplant, but there are also unusual white varieties. And there are different types: Asian (thin fruits), Italian, and mini (good for container gardening).

Eggplant is self-pollinating. Soak the seeds prior to using. Harvest when the fruit turns shiny before seeds have formed. Fruits can also be harvested when half of their mature size. Leave a small piece of stem attached to prolong storage.

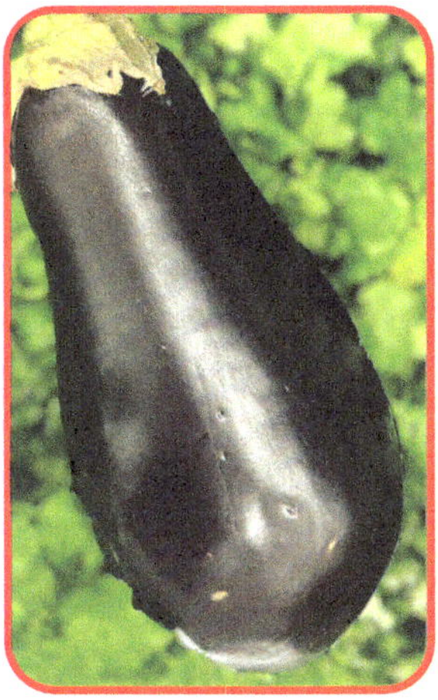

PEPPER

There are many different types of peppers:

- ***Bell/sweet***
- ***Hot*** (Scoville units: jalapeno, cayenne, serrano, habanero)
- ***Frying/cubanelle***
- ***Mini lunchbox/snack***
- ***Ornamental*** (not edible)

One of the best things about peppers is all their pretty colors – green, red, orange, yellow, purple, and chocolate. They make salads and any culinary dish beautiful. Green is the unripe color, which has a crisper taste compared to once they have ripened. Peppers need heat to germinate, otherwise, they will not do well overall. But after true leaves form, exposure to colder nighttime temperatures for a couple of weeks will yield more fruits.

Peppers are self-pollinating, so they can be grown on your lanai. They are sensitive to cold, and flowers will fall off if temperatures are below 60°. They need heavy fertilizer, but keep nitrogen somewhat low to produce flowers.

If picked when green (unripe), peppers will keep producing. But once ripened (red or other colors), they will be sweeter or hotter (depending on variety) and contain higher vitamin levels. Do not touch the seeds of hot peppers, since they are irritating to eyes and skin.

One year, as the weather progressed into the heat of the summer and my peppers finally succumbed to pests (coming off the nearby tomatoes), I cut them back to 2" stalks in order to get ready to pull them out. But I did not get to it right away, and the pepper plants regrew. I got another crop out of them in the fall!

There are many peppers to try. Below are the varieties that I have grown successfully here in Florida in containers. Most were grown on my lanai, except for the heirloom varieties. The color explosion that year was phenomenal. 'Liberty Belle' is a smaller variety that did exceptionally well in containers.

PEPPERS						
Description	**Color**	**Fruit Size**	**Plant Ht.**	**Hybr or OP**	**Days**	**Disease Resist.**
Colored Sweet Peppers						
King Arthur: Umatched for it's large fruit set and eary maturity, sweet crunchy. Performs well under a variety of conditions.	Red	Large 4½x4½"	22"	Hyb	61	Tolerant to most diseases
Red Knight; Large, early, green-to-red pepper, fruity and sweet.	Red	Large 4½x4½"	22"	Hyb	77	BLS, PVY
Liberty Belle: Very sweet attractive yellow-orange. Dwarf variety for containers. High yielding, can withstand heat.	Golden-Orange	Large 4-5"x3-4"	20"	Hyb	73-78	TMV
Early Summer: Beautiful, golden-yellow fruits on strong plants with very impressive yields.	Yellow	Large 4-5x4-5"	24"	Hyb	70-75	Excellent
Merlot: Rich, gourmet eye-appeal and very sweet flavor. High-yielding plants with lush foliage mature early and are adaptable to weather.	Purple	Large 5x4"	18-24"	Hyb	68	TMV, Bacterial Leaf Spot
Frying Peppers						
Biscayne (improved Cubanelle): Fruits that have thicker walls, earlier maturity, more prolific yields, and sweeter flavor than older open-pollinated types.	Light green	Large 5" long	24-30"	Hyb	63	
Heirloom Peppers (outdoors only)						
California Wonder Sweet Bell: Deep green to red, thick-walled with an attractive glossy flesh. A nice stuffer with high yields. Good for outdoor containers.	Green-Red	Large 4x4"	24-30"	OP (heir-loom)	75	
Golden Calwonder Sweet Bell: Fruits ripen to a beautiful golden-yellow color. Good for outdoor containers.	Yellow	Large 4x4"	24-30"	OP (heir-loom)	72	

SQUASH

There are two types of squashes. Summer squashes are thin-skinned and include yellow squash, zucchini, and pattypan. They are bush forms. Winter squashes are hard-skinned and include acorn, butternut, and spaghetti. They can be either bush forms (good for containers) or vining, the latter of which need a trellis if growing in containers.

Squash are insect-pollinated, so they must be grown outdoors. They can be difficult to transplant, but being careful not to disturb the roots, I never had problems. You could also try peat pots or direct sow.

Squash needs plenty of water and fertilizer. They are prone to the squash bug and the squash vine borer (which results in wilting). You can cover the plants (using outdoor row covers) to prevent pests until blossoms occur.

Female blossoms appear before the male and, therefore, fall off if there are no males to pollinate them. However, the flowers are edible and considered a delicacy, often stuffed with cheese, so it is a good use of those extraneous female flowers.

Pick summer squashes young for the best taste (too old and they become bitter) and to keep producing. Winter squashes are ready when the stems are dry. Leave 1" of the stem for best storage. They last many months if cured (10 days in the sun) and properly stored.

Butternut squash in the garden

Summer Zucchini , Yellow

Winter Butternut, Spaghetti, Acorn

TOMATO

The most popular vegetable of all! And the most difficult to grow in terms of problems.

There are several sizes of fruits - large, medium (plum or patio), and cherry/grape. And just like peppers, various colored tomatoes are beautiful in culinary dishes. They include red, orange, yellow, green, purple, and chocolate.

Tomatoes are self-pollinating, which means you can grow them on your lanai or even in your Florida room. They tolerate cold better than most warm-season vegetables and will survive a mild frost. Blossoming stops when temperatures exceed 70o at night (about 90o during the day). Hence, the reason they are not grown in summer. Varieties bred for "high heat and humidity" have a better chance of lasting longer but still will probably not make it through the summer. Cherry tomatoes will do better than larger tomatoes. However, diseases will probably become a problem anyhow as the summer progresses.

Heirloom varieties are tough to grow in Florida. For that reason, sometimes you can find grafted plants to help with disease resistance. There is a variety called 'Everglades,' which some consider native because it is very well adapted to our environment, has good disease resistance, and may survive in all seasons. It is a scraggly large plant and can be grown in a container. Fruits are smaller, like berries.

DETERMINATE VS. INDETERMINATE

There are two types of tomatoes, based on their form - determinate (bush) and indeterminate (vining).

Determinates stay smaller and bushier, so they are best for container gardening. Indeterminates quickly get out of control in terms of size. You can limit their height by cutting off the top of the stem at a height you feel is manageable.

Also, with indeterminate tomatoes, you will need to prune out the suckers. These are branches that try to form in the middle of a branch and the main stem, and they suck the energy out of that branch.

Another difference between the two forms is that determinate varieties put out their fruit all at once, whereas indeterminate will keep going and going and going (until frost or disease takes them out). Although we have two warm growing seasons (spring and fall), rather than the one (summer) in most of the rest of the country, these growing seasons tend to be shorter. Therefore, determinate tomatoes generally go to the end of the season here anyway. I used to grow indeterminate, but even in my outdoor garden, I eventually switched to determinate because they were easier to care for. And in my lanai containers, that is now the only type I grow.

PROPER TRANSPLANTING

When transplanting into your next size container or outdoors, take advantage of an interesting feature. Plant up to the first set of leaves. Adventitious roots will then form along the buried bottom portion of the stem, making the plant stronger. You may sometimes see these roots starting, they appear as tiny bumps. I have removed the topsoil in the photo below so you can see the roots that have formed. If you have leggy tomatoes, you can also lay them on their sides in a trench and cover them with soil. They will eventually right themselves above the soil line, but the adventitious roots will form underground, strengthening the plant.

If you plant multiple plants in a space, plant so that their leaves touch—they have been shown to do better!

GROWING AND HARVESTING

Tomatoes need plenty of water and fertilizer. There are many fertilizer brands specifically made for tomatoes. And certain types of tomatoes will need pruning as they grow. Tomatoes will continue ripening after removal from the vine. If you know a frost is coming, pick any tomatoes that are full-sized, put them on your counter, and wait for them to turn color.

TOMATO PROBLEMS

Tomatoes are prone to a pest called the tomato hornworm, which, as the name implies, has a green "horn." It blends in well with the stem of the plant and can be missed, but it can decimate a plant quickly. If you see small white bumps on its back, leave it - they are parasitic wasp eggs that will eat the hornworm and many other bad insects in your garden.

No more blossoms? If it is not due to high temperatures, as mentioned above, there are other potential reasons. Be sure you are not using a fertilizer with high nitrogen, which will put out foliage at the expense of flowers. Check for pests such as thrips. Make sure your plants are getting enough sun and are getting the right amount of water. Also, it may be due to the life cycle of the plant being done, particularly with determinate plants. This can happen if you buy a plant in the very early spring that is already loaded with tomatoes.

Tomatoes are the most popular vegetable grown, but also one of the hardest to grow in terms of the sheer number of disease problems that can occur. Below is a chart showing diseases that tomatoes can get. Further below, you will see charts showing some tomato varieties that I have grown and what they have been bred to prevent.

TOMATO DISEASES			
Code	**Disease**	**Type**	**Symptoms**
A	Anthracnose	Fungal	Black lesions on fruit and leaves.
BS	Bacterial Spot	Bacterial	Small raised scab lesions, some shot-hole marks.
BW	Bacterial Wilt	Bacterial	Complete wilting.
F (1-3)	Fusarium Wilt	Fungal	Lower leaves turn bright yellow, then wilt.
S	Grey leaf spot	Fungal	Blocky spores with eventual blight.
N	Nematodes	Pest	Wilting plants.
SB	Southern Blight	Fungal	Wilting without yellowing first. Hot/humid weather.
TS	Target spot	Fungal	Small legions (sometimes cracked in a star pattern) with concentric rings.
TYLCV	Tomato Yellow Leaf Curl	Viral	Yellow leaves with green veins. Mostly on indeterminate varieties.
V	Verticillium Wilt	Fungal	V-shaped lesions on lower leaves. Uneven wilting in the plant, may recover overnight.

Diseases, especially fungal, can be reduced by pruning leaves up from the base so they do not touch the soil. I usually prune mine up about 1 foot.

Another common problem is cracking, which is usually due to uneven watering.

Blossom end rot occurs with a calcium deficiency. Commonly, it is thought that it is a fertilizer deficiency. But it can also be due to too much water (removing the calcium), too little water (calcium cannot be taken up), cold (which slows the plant from taking up fertilizer nutrients), or incorrect pH (which reduces the ability of the plant to take up nutrients).

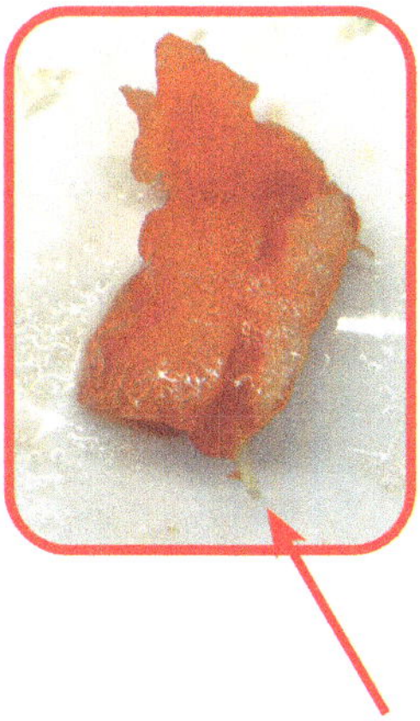

If you slice into your tomato and find a tiny white stem-like structure, it could be that a seed has sprouted inside the fruit! This can happen if the fruit is overripe.

GREAT TOMATO TASTE

Can't grow a tasty tomato in Florida? **Ugh - WHY?** I was a "snowbird" for the first few years in Florida, spending summers in New England and fall/winter/spring in Florida. While in New England in the summer, I grew Celebrity tomatoes, always one of the top winners in my taste tests with neighbors. I then took that exact same seed packet down to Florida and planted it outside for the fall season, growing the same way I always had. My husband and I did a taste test ourselves at the end of the season, and we both said, "What happened? It is tasteless!"

So, what is different? One thing is our Floridian soil, which is primarily sand. Make sure you add compost if you are growing outdoors. If using containers, ensure that your container mix has it, or add it yourself. Water can be different, and sunlight is much more intense, but I am not sure those are major factors.

Below are some suggestions to try. The first few are general best practices for growing tomatoes anyway. But I personally have found that my results improved following the last two, regarding soil/mix and water.

- ***Tomato variety.*** Cherry and smaller tomatoes are sweeter than larger tomatoes. Make sure your variety description includes "sweet" rather than "storage." Variety and genetics probably play the biggest role in sweetness.
- ***Sun.*** Make sure you are getting full sun and, therefore, lots of lush foliage (for photosynthesis and sugars).
- ***Prune.*** Remove suckers to reduce the number of fruits, concentrating flavor in the remaining fruit.
- ***Harvest.*** Pick at the peak of ripeness, when sugars are highest.
- ***Soil/Mix.*** Add plenty of compost, and fertilize regularly. Enhancements of beneficial microbes, kelp/seaweed extracts, enzymes, and vitamins/minerals may help with nutrient and sugar uptake.
- ***Water.*** Back off on watering after fruits appear and towards harvest time, which will concentrate sugars.

Here are some tomatoes that I have grown in Florida. I grew the more disease-resistant ones in my outdoor garden, however, that did not make them immune to pests, particularly the lubber. As a result, I now grow only in containers on my lanai.

TOMATOES - LARGE FRUIT								
Description	**Color**	**Fruit Size**	**Plant Ht.**	**Stake**	**Det/ In-det**	**Hybr or OP**	**Days**	**Disease Resist.**
Celebrity Plus: Semi-determinate variety with outstanding flavor. Improved version of the AAS winner, Celebrity.	Red	Med-Large 7-8 oz.	48"+	Y	Det	Hyb	70	V F(3) N T A St TSWV
Charger: High yielding, brilliant red fruits, very firm with good flavor, high sugar, low acid. Strong disease resistance ("takes charge of disease").	Red	Med-Large	24"	Y	Det	Hyb	76	V F3 A St YLCV
Dixie: Plump, delicious and juicy fruit. Bred to perform well in hot, humid climates.	Red	Larger 11-12 oz.	med	Y	Det	Hyb	80-90	V F3 A GLS
Florida 47: Originally bred for commercial production for using fruits green or vine ripened red. Heavy yields and highly disease resistant.	Red	Large 10 oz.	med	Y	Det	Hyb	75	V F A St
Galahad: Fantastic flavor and impressive disease resistance including for the deep South.	Red	Large 7-12 oz.	med	Y	Det	Hyb	69	F3 GLS LB N TSWV V
Grand Marshall: An excellent choice for the South for its ability to set fruit in the heat, and improved disease resistance.	Red	Large 10-14 oz.	med	Y	Det	Hyb	78	AS F2 V GLS TYLCV
Heatmaster: Great fresh, plus good shelf life. Firm fruits. Bred for hot/humid climates (sets fruits under higher temps).	Red	Med-Large 7 oz.	36"	Y	Det	Hyb	78-80	VF F N T A St
Red Snapper: Attractive deep red firm fruits full of great tomato flavor. Sets well in the heat, high yielder. Developed with UFL.	Red	Med-Large 8-12 oz.	med-tall	Y	Det	Hyb	70-75	V F2 A St
SkyWay: Large beefsteak with good flavor and broad disease resistance for the South.	Red	Large 8-12 oz.	36"	Y	Det	Hyb	78	F3 ToANV V N TSWV TYLCV
Tasti-Lee 2: Extra firm rich red fruits with high lycopene content that provides excellent flavor. High yielding, hot climates. Developed by UFL.	Red	Med-Large 6-9 oz.	36"	Y	Det	Hyb	75	V F3 YLCV

TOMATOES - MEDIUM FRUIT (PATIO/PLUM)							
Description	**Color**	**Fruit Size**	**Plant Ht.**	**Det/ Indet**	**Hybr or OP**	**Days**	**Disease Resist.**
Plum							
Plum Regal: High yields of good-flavored plum tomatoes.	Red	4 oz.	30"	Det	Hyb	75	F2 LB TSWV V EB
Patio							
Little Sicily: Good tasting small slicer (patio sized) with rugose foliage. Great for containers.	Red	Medium 1½"-2"	24-36"	Det	Hyb	60-65	F1
Patio Hybrid: Firm oval fruits with flavorful taste. Rugose leaves. Strong stem, compact.	Red	Medium 1½"-2"	24-36"	Det	Hyb	70	F A St
Taxi: Mild sweet flavored, acid free. Meaty flesh, beautiful color. Excellent fresh. Early, prolific.	Yellow	Medium 1½"-2"	30"	Det	OP	65-70	None

TOMATOES - CHERRY							
Description	**Color**	**Fruit Size**	**Plant Ht.**	**Det/ In-det**	**Hybr or OP**	**Days**	**Dis-ease Resist.**
Cherry, tall indeterminate							
Everglades: Florida "native" with tomato berries (red, blueberry-sized). Full flavor like a large beefsteak. Adapted to Florida's extreme weather.	Red	Cherry ½"	48"	Ind.	OP	90	Good disease resist.
Sweet Million: Long chains of dark red super-sweet terrific tasting tomatoes. Early, vigorous plants with excellent disease resistance.	Red	1-1½"	Tall!	Ind.	Hyb	60	FT
SunSugar: Golden yellow fruits with super sugary sweetness, and superb texture that resist cracking. Heavy, early crops.	Golden Yellow	½ oz.	Tall!	Ind.	Hyb	62	F ToMV
Cherry, for containers							
Patio Choice Hybrid: Compact, cascading plants produce generous amount of 2-3 oz bright red, juicy, delicious cherry size fruits. Great for containers.	Red	1½" (2-3 oz.)	36"	Det	Hyb	50-60	
Patio Choice Yellow: Bright yellow fruits on small, cascading plants with prolific yields of delicious fruits. Perfect for containers.	Yellow	1" (2 oz.)	24-28"	Det	Hyb	50-60	
Red Racer: Good sweet/acid balance, big in taste. Fruit in clusters. Early producer. AAS winer.	Red	Cherry 1½"	36"	Det	Hyb	57	V F2 N St ToMV
Ruby Crush: Oval shaped. Good sugar/acid balance. Resists cracking.	Red	Grape 1"	36"	Det	Hyb	60	F T St
Tiny Tim: Great for salads. Early. Tree-like with rugose leaves.	Red	Cherry ¾"	18-36"	Det	Hyb	60	
Cherry, dwarf/hydroponics							
Micro Tom: Flavorful, prolific, with rugose leaves. Hydropoinics, or can be used in hanging containers. No staking. Developed by University of Florida.	Red	Cherry ½"	6"	Det	Hyb	50-60	F St
Red Robin: Extra sweet, with rugose leaves. Small size is excellent for containers, hydroponics, or hanging baskets. No need to stake.	Red	Cherry 1"	12"	Det	Hyb	55	

QUICK REFERENCE CHART

WARM SEASON VEGETABLES				
Vegetable	Design		Seeding & Transplanting	Trans. Diff.
	Family	Poll.		
Beans '- Pole (vining) - Bush - Snap/string - Shell - Filet (haricot verts) - Lima	Legume	None	• Direct sow, or be careful with transplanting (most are started directly in soil or containers). • Good for succession planting. • Microbial inoculants may increase yields in poor soils (generally not needed for FL).	H
Corn **Sweet:** - Sugary (SU) - Sugar enhanced (SE - firm/ sweet) - Supersweet (SH2, tender/ sweet) - Synergistic (SYN, combines SE and SH2) Field/ornamental (cornmeal) Popcorn (starchy) Old fashioined (open pollinated, tough)	Corn	Wind	• Colors include white, yellow, bicolor, multi. • Some kernels seeds are coated with a fungicide, which negates them from being organic and may affect good fungi in the soil. • Usually direct-seeded in warm soil. • Plant on north side of garden (tall). • Plant in 4-row short blocks to ensure wind pollination. • Avoid cross-pollination if growing different types, by either distance or succession planting every 2 weeks.	H
Cucumber - Slicing - Pickling (thinner skins) - Burpless/seedless - English/Japanese (super crisp)	Cucumber	Insect or Self (parthe-nocar-pic)	• Bush or vine forms. • Burpless = seedless, as long as no corss-pollination occurs. • "Gynoecious" varieties have only female flowers, thus producing more fruit. • Good for succession planting.	H

QUICK REFERENCE CHART

WARM SEASON VEGETABLES					
Growing	Plant Care				Harvesting
	Light	Water	Nutrients	Pests/Diseases	
• Although a warm weather crop, it may make it through warm Floridian winters.	S	Moderate	Moderate (but low nitrogen, due to fixing)	- Bean beetle - Bean roller - Rust disease	• Best flavor comes from young plants. • Pole beans may taster better (sweet, tender) than bush. • Many types of beans can be eaten raw, as well as cooked. • Harvest ontinually to keep producing.
• Shake plant to increase pollination.	S	Heavy (shallow rooted)	Heavy (keep fertilizing)	- Corn earworm (silks) - Corn borer (stems) - Squirrels, birds, raccoons (try using foil ribbon that reflects in the light and blows in the wind, or fake owls)	• When silk ends are brown and kernels are milky inside (too watery = not ready). • Pick in morning for highest sugar. • Eat fresh that day (turns to starch within a day after picking).
• Parthenocarpic varieties set fruit without pollination, good for lanais, and they are seedless.	S	Heavy (otherwise, bitter fruit)	Heavy (keep fertilizing)	- Cucumber beetle - Powdery mildew	• Pick small for best flavor. Too large = bitter. • Keep picking to keep producing.

QUICK REFERENCE CHART

WARM SEASON VEGETABLES				
Vegetable	Design		Seeding & Transplanting	Trans. Diff.
	Family	Poll.		
Eggplant '- Asian (thin fruits) - Italian - Mini	Night-shade	Self	• Colors include purple and white. • Soak seeds prior to planting. • Compact and mini fruit varieties exist for container gardening.	L
Melon - Honeydew - Musk (cantaloupe) - Watermelon	Cucumber	Insect		H
Pepper - Bell/sweet - Hot (jalpeno, cayenne, habanero) - Frying/Cubanelle - Mini lunchbox/snack - Ornamental (not edible)	Night-shade	Self	• Beautiful colors include green (unripe), red, orange, yellow, purple, chocolate. • Need heat to germinate. But after true leaves form, expose to cold for2 weeks for more fruits. • Plants like to touch. • Flowers will drop in low heat.	L
Pumpkin	Cucumber	Insect	• Besides the standard orange, other colors include white, gold, and multi-colored. • Some mini pumpkin fruits exist for containers.	H

QUICK REFERENCE CHART

WARM SEASON VEGETABLES					
Growing	Plant Care				Harvesting
	Light	Water	Nutrients	Pests/Diseases	
	S	Heavy	Moderate	- Flea beetles	• Harvest when fruit turns shiny, before seeds have formed. Fruits can also be harvested when half of mature size. • Leave a small piece of stem on to prolong storage.
• Need space for vines to grow. Very hard to grow in containers. • Keep fruit off soil. Place on board or mulch. If growing vertically on trellis, use stocking or net to hold up fruit, tie to trellis.	S	Heavy (but too much = watery fruits and less flavor, back off week before harvest)	Moderate	- Aphids - Slugs	• Harvest when exterior turns ripe color (ie., musk melon = buff).
• Sensitive to cold, flowers will fall off if temperatures go below 60°.	S	Moderate	Heavy (except N)		• Green = unripe. Colors = ripe, sweeter, higher vitamin levels. • If picked when green, will keep producing. • Don't touch seeds of hot peppers, irritating to eyes and skin. • Hot peppers are rated by Scoville units.
• Needs lots of space for long vines. • Need a long growing season.	S	Heavy	Moderate	- Squash beetle	• Harvest when stem turns brown. • Cure in sun for 1 week..

QUICK REFERENCE CHART

WARM SEASON VEGETABLES				
Vegetable	**Design**		**Seeding & Transplanting**	**Trans. Diff.**
	Family	**Poll.**		
Squash - Summer (Zucchini, Yellow) - Winter (Acorn, Butternut, Spaghetti)	Cucumber	Insect	• Bush (best for containers) or vine forms. • Needs warm soil for transplanting.	H
Tomato Fruit: - Large/beefsteak - Roma - Patio - Cherry/grape Types: - Determinate - Indeterminate - Heirloom - Grafted - 'Everglades'	Night-shade	Self	• Many beautiful colors including red, orange, yellow, green, purple, chocolate. • Determinate (bush) types set fruit all at once, good for containers. • Indeterminate (vine) forms need a trellis, and continually produce fruits. • Heirlooms are tough to grow in Florida due to their lack of disease resistance, but sometimes are grafted onto strong root stock. • 'Everglades' behaves like a native, and has small berry-like fruits. • Plant up to 1st set of leaves for stronger plants.	L

QUICK REFERENCE CHART

WARM SEASON VEGETABLES					
Growing	Plant Care				Harvesting
	Light	Water	Nutrients	Pests/Diseases	
• Falling blossoms are due to female blossoms appearing before male.	S-PS	Heavy	Heavy	- Squash beetle - Squash vine borer - Powdery mildew	• Flowers are edible, a delicacy. • Pick summer squashes young for best taste (too old = bitter) and to keep producing. • Winter squashes are ready when sems are dry. Leave 1" of stem on. • Cure winter varieties for 10 days in sun.
• Will stop flowering in high heat (over 70° at night). • Cherry tomatoes may make it further into the summer season. • Prune suckers on indeterminate varieties.	S	Heavy	Heavy (keep fertilizing)	- Tomato horn-worm - Cracking (uneven watering) - Catfacing (too cold, too much N) - Blossom end rot (uneven watering, heat/cold damage during blossom set)	• Will continue to ripen after picking.

PART 3 – RECIPES

COOKING WITH VEGETABLES

Some vegetables are cooked, others are eaten raw. Surprisingly, some that you think need to be cooked can actually be eaten raw or al dente, which means they are barely cooked and still somewhat crisp, which better holds on to their nutrients.

Regardless of how you cook a vegetable meal, presentation can enhance any dish. Use colorful vegetables, such as purple, yellow, and orange carrots, instead of just orange. Use yellow, orange, and purple tomatoes along with red. Peppers come in a variety of colors as well. Lettuce comes in tasty and pretty red varieties. Squashes are colorful yellows and oranges. If using green vegetables, place them on a pretty plate. Or add edible organically raised flowers such as nasturtiums on the plate (which also look pretty growing in your garden or container with your vegetable crop). Add herbs for garnish. Decorating can make even the simplest dish look impressive!

The recipes in this book are intended to be easy for those who do not wish to spend long hours in the kitchen. Also, most of these recipes can be customized to your tastes. If you want more of a certain ingredient, for example, just add it.

The recipes are broken into the following categories: 1) appetizers, 2) main dishes, 3) soups, salads, and sandwiches, and 4) sides. They are alphabetical within those categories.

APPETIZERS

CAPRESE SKEWERS

When tomatoes are ready on the vine, there are so many ways to use them. One of my family favorites is Caprese salad, using larger tomatoes.

This recipe is a little different, though, because it uses cherry tomatoes on skewers, which are great as a hand-held appetizer when having guests over or for driveway parties. If you vary it with colorful red, orange, yellow, and purple tomatoes, it creates a very pretty presentation. Use fresh basil for the skewers for an intoxicating aroma. You can also add tortellini if you would like something more filling.

Use the smaller 6" sized wooden skewers, which hold 7 pieces per skewer. Two skewers per person is usually sufficient, but it will vary depending on how many other appetizers you are serving as well.

INGREDIENTS [8 skewers]

8	*Wooden skewers*
24	*Cherry tomatoes in red, orange, yellow, purple*
16	*Small mozzarella balls*
16	*Fresh basil leaves, plus sprigs for decoration*
16	*Cheese tortellini pieces, cooked (optional)*
	Marinade
¼ cup	*Olive oil*
2 tbsp	*Vinegar*
1 tbsp	*Honey*
1 tbsp	*Dried basil*
1 tsp	*Garlic, chopped*
½ tsp	*Salt*

COOKING INSTRUCTIONS

1. Whisk all marinade ingredients in a bowl.
2. Most skewer recipes say to thread first and then marinate, and you are welcome to do that, but we have found that the wooden skewers themselves always tend to get marinade all over them, making it messier for guests to handle. We prefer the following method instead: marinating first, then threading later. It is a little messier for the cook, but it is also the best way to get thorough coverage and, thus, the best flavor.
3. Add tomatoes, mozzarella balls, and optionally, cooked tortellini. Stir marinade over pieces.
4. Place in fridge for a minimum of two hours, occasionally stirring to ensure thorough coverage.
5. Thread the skewers. Thread in any order you would like, but this is one pretty option: 1-tomato color1 (which will end up on the bottom), 2-basil leaf, 3-mozzarella, 4-tomato color2 or tortellini, 5-basil leaf, 6-mozzarella, 7-tomato color3. Place completed skewers on a serving plate.
6. Drizzle a small amount of remaining marinade over top, staying away from the end of each skewer. Place additional sprigs of basil around for decoration.

CHARCUTERIE WITH VEGETABLES

Charcuterie boards are the ultimate appetizer for guests. There are so many combinations that can be used to create beautiful arrangements. And a pretty board on which to showcase everything, along with cute little dishes for accompaniments, adds to the setting. If you do not have a board, use a pretty serving platter. Presentation is the name of the game here.

Besides the usual cheeses and meats, this recipe also incorporates vegetables for vegans, vegetarians, and those who wish to eat healthy at a party. You do not have to incorporate everything from this list – just pick items that fit your board and ingredients that go together from a culinary perspective.

INGREDIENTS [4 servings]

Main ingredients

(amounts may vary depending on the size of your board, but below are typical)

3-4 Cheeses of various shapes and colors – white cheddar, orange cheddar, gouda, brie, goat, Roquefort, string cheese

2 Meats such as prosciutto, soppressata, genoa

2 Cracker types

1 French bread, sliced and toasted

Raw fruits and vegetables

Tomatoes, cherry, colored

Cucumbers, seedless, sliced

Carrots, colored, sliced into sticks

Celery sticks

Asparagus, raw

Apples, sliced

Grapes

Fillers (in bowls)

Whipped feta or creamy dip

Mozzarella balls, cherry tomato sized

Hummus

Olives (without pits)

Pickles (gherkin)

Nuts

Accompaniments (in tiny dishes)

Stone ground mustard

Honey mustard

Honey

Jam

Garnishes

Rosemary sprigs

Microgreens

COOKING INSTRUCTIONS

Preparation:

- ***Slice hard cheeses like cheddar and gouda.*** It looks cute to have a chunk of cheese with a knife in it, but it really is not practical for guests to easily cut. Cut each cheese variety into a different shape – rectangles, triangles, cubes.
- ***For soft cheeses like goat cheese and Roquefort, on the other hand, keep whole and insert a small knife.*** For brie, remove the top piece of white rind, so the interior can be more easily accessed with a small spoon.
- ***Make "flowers" out of the meat slices.*** Take a small shot glass and rim it with round meat, overlapping slices, then remove and place edge-side up. Although this is pretty, it is difficult for guests to pick apart. A more practical option is to fold the meats in quarters. Softer, flexible meats, like prosciutto pieces, can be scrunched.
- ***Make mini skewers.*** For example, wrap a piece of prosciutto around provolone string cheese. Or a piece of soppressata around cheddar string cheese. Combine a cherry tomato, mozzarella ball, and a piece of basil.
- ***Asparagus can indeed be eaten raw.*** But if you want it cooked al dente, place spears in boiling water for 2-4 minutes, then quickly place in cool water.

- ***Be sure to slice apples right before serving since they will turn brown otherwise.*** A trick to prevent that is to lightly brush them with lemon juice.
- ***Pull grapes off the stems.*** Yes, it looks quintessentially nice, but again, it is not very practical for guests to pull from and possibly mess up the entire board.
- ***To make a whipped feta dip, blend 8 oz.*** crumbled feta, 4 oz. whipped cream cheese, 2 oz. olive oil, 1 clove minced garlic, and 1 teaspoon oregano.

Presentation tips:

- ***Completely fill your board, making sure items are touching without empty space.***
- ***Place the bowls and tiny dishes on the board first.*** Everything else will work around them.
- ***Place good food combinations next to each other.*** For instance, honey goes well with goat cheese and Roquefort. Cherry tomatoes go well with mozzarella balls. Carrots work with whipped feta or a creamy dip. Honey mustard is great with meats and cheddar.
- ***When arranging your items on the board, think of curves.*** Fan bread, crackers, meats, and cheeses out in a curved manner, perhaps around the round bowls.
- ***Pile items up in multiple horizontal layers.*** And place some items upright, like bread, crackers, and cheese.
- ***Color, color, color.*** Place throughout so that not all the bland items are next to each other.
- ***Fill in any gaps or in several areas along the outside rim with a garnish such as rosemary or microgreens.***
- ***Place small serving tongs on the side so guests do not have to pick through the board items.*** Place tiny spoons or forks in the dish items.

CUCUMBER AND FETA DIP

This is a healthy vegetarian appetizer using fresh, crisp cucumbers. The red onions and fresh dill add to the presentation. It pairs especially well with pita crackers.

INGREDIENTS [4 servings]

½ cup	*Cucumber, seeds removed, sliced, and cut into small pieces*
¼ cup	*Red onion, diced*
½ cup	*Feta cheese, crumbled*
½ cup	*Sour cream*
½ cup	*Cream cheese*
1 tbsp	*Lemon juice*
1 tbsp	*Dill*
Taste	*Salt*

COOKING INSTRUCTIONS

1. Place the feta, sour cream, cream cheese, and lemon juice in a bowl. Using a mixer or immersion blender, blend until mixed but lumpy with small pieces of feta.
2. Add the cucumber, red onion, dill, and salt, and hand mix.
3. Place in a pretty bowl and garnish with fresh dill sprigs.
4. Place the bowl on a pretty plate and surround it with crackers.

PEPPER & ONION FLATBREAD

A great healthy, vegetarian appetizer. This is made on a flatbread (we use a gluten-free version), but it could also be made on a pizza crust. Colorful peppers and onions are showcased and topped with high- quality olive oil, fresh parsley or microgreens, and crumbled goat cheese (you may also substitute feta cheese).

INGREDIENTS [4 servings]

2	*Flatbreads, 8″ x 8″ (makes 8 slices)*
1 each	*Colored bell peppers – red, orange, yellow*
¼ cup	*Red onion*
4 oz.	*Crumbled goat cheese (or feta)*
3 tbsp	*Fresh parsley leaves or microgreens*
2 tbsp	*Olive oil*
1 tsp	*Salt*

COOKING INSTRUCTIONS

1. Cook flatbread according to package directions.
2. Cut peppers and onions into strips, approximately 3/8″ wide and 1½″ to 2″ long.
3. Microwave peppers and onions for 30 seconds on high to soften slightly.
4. Place on flatbread.
5. Drizzle olive oil and vinegar over flatbread.
6. Place in 350° pre-heated oven and cook for approximately 5 minutes until peppers and onions are slightly soft.
7. Remove from oven. Sprinkle with goat cheese, parsley leaves, and salt.
8. Use a pizza cutter wheel to slice into 4 square pieces. Use a spatula to move to a pretty plate or platter.

TACO CUPS

These are very simple to make and are always a hit with guests at driveway parties. Although an appetizer, they are somewhat substantial. We prefer to make a mild version since some people do not care for spicy foods, but you can make them to your own taste. We find that 2 of these per person is about the right amount if serving other appetizers as well.

INGREDIENTS [16 pieces]

16	*Mini nacho shells, pre-formed into cups*
1 lb.	*Ground beef*
1	*Sweet onion*
1 pkg.	*Taco seasoning (or make your own with red pepper, etc.)*
1 cup	*Finely shredded Mexican cheese*
2 tbsp	*Cilantro leaves, fresh, cut finely*
¼ cup	*Sour cream*

COOKING INSTRUCTIONS

1. Dice the sweet onion and place it in a frying pan. Add the beef and cook thoroughly until browned.
2. Stir in the taco seasoning until the meat mixture is coated.
3. Remove from heat. Fill each shell with the mixture.
4. Top with shredded cheese. Broil for 1-2 minutes until cheese is melted.
5. Add a small amount of sour cream, then top with chopped cilantro.
6. Place on a pretty plate for serving. Scatter cilantro around the plate for decoration.

MAIN DISHES

CHICKEN POT PIE

This dish is reminiscent of a hearty homestyle meal that is especially good in the cooler months. We like to make it with a gluten-free crust and use vegetables such as celery, onion, and carrots, but you can also use traditional peas and carrots.

INGREDIENTS [6 servings]

2	*Pie crusts (can be gluten-free)*
2 cups	*Chicken breasts, cooked and diced*
¼ cup	*Sweet onion, quartered and sliced*
¼ cup	*Carrots, diced*
¼ cup	*Celery, diced (or peas)*
3 tbsp	*Butter*
3 tbsp	*Flour (can be gluten-free)*
1½ cup	*Chicken broth*
2 tsp	*Parsley*
taste	*Salt, pepper*

COOKING INSTRUCTIONS

1. Cook chicken breasts until done, then dice.
2. Melt butter in a saucepan, then mix in flour. Add chicken broth and stir until thickened.
3. Stir in onion, celery, and carrots. Cook over medium-high heat until slightly tender, approximately 10 minutes or less if you prefer your vegetables more al dente.
4. Add parsley and salt.
5. Pour the mixture into the bottom pie crust.

6. Flatten the sides of the top crust, then place on top of the pie. This will probably be messy, and you may not get it to stay in one piece. Use a touch of water on the dough to smooth out imperfections as much as possible.
7. Use your finger to join the outer rim of the top pie shell to the bottom. Then, use a fork to make indentations around the outer rim. Make knife slits in the top for the steam to escape.
8. Sprinkle with parsley.
9. Cook at 350° for approximately 30 minutes.

GINGER CHICKEN WITH CORN ON THE COB

This is a recipe that my husband created and has made many times over the years. It is fast and easy if cooked in the microwave, but it is also great on the grill or in the oven. Do you know the best way to cook corn? Read below.

INGREDIENTS [2 servings]

2	*Chicken breasts*
	Marinade
¼ cup	*Soy sauce (lite, if possible)*
¼ cup	*Olive oil*
2 tbsp	*Honey*
1/3 cup	*Ginger (sliced crystallized, if possible)*
2 tbsp	*Rosemary*
2 tbsp	*Scallions (or shallots)*
1 clove	*Garlic, crushed or chopped finely*
	Corn on the Cob
4 ears	*Corn, shucked*
1 stick	*Butter*
Taste	*Salt*

COOKING INSTRUCTIONS

Ginger Chicken

1. Mix all marinade ingredients together.
2. Place chicken in a microwaveable dish, coating thoroughly with marinade.
3. Refrigerate for a minimum of 2 hours (can also be done overnight). Turn over halfway through to ensure coating.
4. Cook chicken until done in the microwave at 50% power for approximately 15 minutes, or on the grill or in the oven.
5. Remove the chicken from the dish.
6. Microwave the remaining marinade until it thoroughly boils (since the raw meat was originally in the marinade).
7. Plate the chicken, then pour some of the marinade over each. Set aside any remaining marinade in a gravy boat for use at the table.

Corn on the Cob

1. Corn on the cob can be made by boiling or on the grill, but the easiest and best way to preserve the plumpness is to steam it. Add water to cover the bottom inch of a large pan.
2. Place the shucked corn ears in the pan upright, cover, and steam for 5-10 minutes.
3. And the easiest way to thoroughly coat with butter? Place a stick of butter on a butter dish, and roll each ear in the stick.
4. Add salt and enjoy!

PASTA CHICKEN SALAD

I love to grow peppers in all colors of the rainbow. And this pasta salad shows them off beautifully! If you are a vegetarian, you can remove the chicken and substitute broccoli, arugula, or another type of vegetable instead. This dish is an easy and pretty potluck dish.

INGREDIENTS [8 servings]

2 cups	*Penne pasta (will be 5-6 cups after cooking)*
1 lb.	*Chicken tenders, cooked and diced (makes 2 cups)*
1 ea.	*Red, orange, and yellow bell peppers, diced (makes 1 cup total)*
¼ cup	*Red onion, diced*
½ cup	*Celery, diced*
1 tbsp	*Parsley, fresh flat-leaf, cut up*
1/3 cup	*Olive oil*
1 tbsp	*Parmesan cheese, shaved*
1 tsp	*Salt*
½ tsp	*Pepper*

(optional for creamy version)

6 tbsp	*Mayonnaise*
2 tbsp	*Sour cream*

COOKING INSTRUCTIONS

1. Cook pasta according to package directions. Wait until the pasta has cooled before continuing.
2. Set aside 2 tablespoons of peppers, 1 teaspoon of parsley, and parmesan cheese. Mix all other ingredients together.
3. Top the center with remaining peppers, parsley, and parmesan cheese for decoration.
4. Serve cold.

SALMON WITH CUCUMBER SAUCE

Salmon is very healthy to begin with, and this crisp, cool cucumber topping just adds to its benefits. Serve it with any of the healthy side dishes found in this book.

The topping can also be made separately and used as a side salad for salmon or other dishes. Just use less of the wet ingredients (to coat the cucumbers rather than as a sauce) and toss with feta.

INGREDIENTS [2 servings]

1	*Salmon fillet (for 2)*
	Topping
1 cup	*Cucumber, peeled, seeds removed, and diced*
2 tbsp	*Sweet onion, diced*
5 tbsp	*Sour cream*
2 tbsp	*Mayonnaise*
2 tbsp	*Lemon juice*
2 tbsp	*Dill, preferably fresh, or 1 tbsp dried*
Taste	*Salt*

COOKING INSTRUCTIONS

1. Mix all the sauce ingredients together. Set aside.
2. Place salmon in a baking dish. Cook in 425° degree oven for approximately 15 minutes or until your preference for the level of doneness, and until topping is slightly browned.
3. Remove from oven, plate, and top with sauce.

STEAK WITH CHEESY SCALLION TOPPING, ROASTED BEANS WITH LEEKS

Steaks are naturally great on the grill. But in Florida, in the heat of the summer, we tend to put aside the grill in favor of using our kitchen oven - in air conditioning! Either way, this topping will enhance your steaks.

Add colorful roasted potatoes on the side, along with some fresh green beans.

STEAK

INGREDIENTS [2 servings]

2	*Steaks (ribeye work well)*
1 tsp	*Salt*
1 tsp	*Pepper*
	Topping
1 stick	*Unsalted butter, softened*
1-2 cups	*Shredded cheddar cheese*
1 tsp	*Mustard, Dijon*
3 tbsp	*Scallions, diced*

COOKING INSTRUCTIONS

1. Mix all topping ingredients together. Set aside.
2. Coat steaks with salt and pepper. In a frying pan, sear steaks over medium heat until browned, approximately 3 minutes on each side. Transfer steaks to a roasting pan.
3. In a 325° pre-heated oven, continue cooking steaks. The amount of time will vary depending on the thickness of your steaks and your desired level of doneness. (Generally, 10 minutes suffices, but watch them carefully to be sure.)
4. Meanwhile, cook beans and potatoes (see below).
5. Plate steak and add a dollop of topping on each. Add potatoes and beans on the side.

COLORFUL ROASTED POTATOES

INGREDIENTS

2 cups	*Colored potatoes – red, white, blue*
2 tbsp	*Olive oil*
1 tbsp	*Chives, fresh, diced*
1 tsp	*Salt*
½ tsp	*Pepper*

COOKING INSTRUCTIONS

1. Chop potatoes (unpeeled) into bite-sized pieces and place in a bowl. Add olive oil. Set aside 1 tsp chives, but add the remainder to the bowl. Toss until potatoes are well coated.
2. Spead out on a cookie sheet in a single layer.
3. Place in a pre-heated 325° oven and cook until tender, approximately 20 minutes. If potatoes are not browned, broil for an additional 3-5 minutes.
4. After plating, add salt, pepper, and remaining chives.

STEAMED GREEN BEANS

INGREDIENTS

½ lb.	*Green/pole beans*
1 tbsp	*Almonds, sliced*
1 tbsp	*Butter*
Taste	*Salt*

COOKING INSTRUCTIONS

1. Cut off the ends of pole beans and place in a saucepan.
2. Bring 1" of water in the saucepan to a boil.
3. Reduce heat to medium, cover, and steam for approximately 10 minutes until softened (but not mushy).
4. Remove from water.
5. Plate, then top with butter and almonds.

TURKEY SAUSAGE, SWEET POTATO, & ONION HASH

This dish is a delicious use of sweet potatoes. It is not too heavy feeling, so it is great for suppertime.

INGREDIENTS [2 servings]

1 lb.	*Ground turkey sausage, spiced*
1 large	*Sweet potato, cubed*
1	*Sweet onion, quarter sliced*
1 cup	*Crumbled feta*
3 tbsp	*Olive oil*

COOKING INSTRUCTIONS

1. Boil pre-cubed sweet potato for approximately 10 minutes until tender, but not so tender that it will fall apart when mixed.
2. Cook turkey sausage in a skillet over medium heat until browned.
3. Add onions and cook until tender.
4. Add sweet potato.
5. Let cool slightly, then top with feta, olive oil, and serve in bowls.

SOUPS, SALADS, AND SANDWICHES

BUTTERNUT SQUASH AND APPLE SOUP

Butternut squash can be prepared in many ways. Our favorites are roasted (cubed), mashed, and in this soup. Although it is hearty and usually considered a fall soup, we do not let that stop us from making it year-round. Presentation at the table makes it appear very upscale (see instructions below).

INGREDIENTS [4 servings]

2 cups	*Butternut squash, peeled, seeds removed, diced*
¾ cup	*Apple, Honey Crisp, or similar if possible*
3 cups	*Vegetable broth (without mushrooms or tomato sauce)*
4 tbsp	*Unsalted sweet cream butter, melted*
½ cup	*Heavy cream*
2 tbsp	*Maple syrup*
½ tsp	*Ground nutmeg*
	Presentation
¼ cup	*Crème fraiche OR heavy cream*
¼ cup	*Apple, diced*
Sprigs	*Thyme*
¼ tsp	*Cloves*

COOKING INSTRUCTIONS

1. Peel squash, remove seeds, and cut into ½″ cubes. If you did not grow your own squash and wish to make life easier, buy the squash already cubed from the grocery store.
2. Peel apple, core, and cut into ½″ cubes.
3. Place vegetable broth in a large saucepan. Add squash and ½ cup diced apple.
4. Bring to a boil, then cook over medium heat until the squash is tender, about 20 minutes. Remove from heat.
5. Using a hand-held (immersion) blender, mix until smooth. If you prefer a regular blender, blend the soup in batches, but it is a much messier method.
6. Add butter, ½ cup cream, maple syrup, and nutmeg.
7. Heat on low for another 10 minutes.
8. Serving suggestion #1 (for each bowl): Pour soup into a water pitcher. Place a dollop of crème fraiche in the bottom of a low soup bowl. Place a few pieces of the apple on top of the crème fraiche, then place a sprig of thyme in the middle of the crème fraiche. Sprinkle with cloves. Place these bowls on the table for each person, so everyone can see how pretty it is. Then pour soup at the table for each person, around the crème fraiche.
9. Serving suggestion #2 (for each bowl): Pour soup into a low bowl. Add a tablespoon of cream in the middle. Take a knife and swirl through the cream so that it leaves a pretty pattern. Sprinkle a small amount of cloves on top.

GREEN SALAD WITH APPLES, CRANBERRIES, WALNUTS

Of course, there are many combinations for making a green salad. I like to have home-grown lettuce on hand, ready for picking when I need it. And I prefer the color that red romaine lettuce brings to a salad, particularly this one, to show off the apples, but any variety may be used.

We serve this as its own course during multi-course meals, along with a nice brown or French bread with honey butter. You could also add chicken to this to make it a complete meal.

INGREDIENTS [2 servings]

1 head	*Lettuce*
1 lb.	*Chicken (optional) - tenders, browned and cooked*
2	*Apples, cored, cut into ¼" slices*
1/8 cup	*Dried cranberries*
2 tbsp	*Walnuts, chopped*
2 tbsp	*Roquefort cheese, crumbled*
Taste	*Salt*

COOKING INSTRUCTIONS

1. Simply place all ingredients on top of some lettuce, serving on individual plates.

GREEN SALAD WITH ORANGES, AVOCADO, RED ONION

Salmon pairs wonderfully with this salad and can be used to make it a complete meal. However, it is also nice as a side dish or if you wish to remain vegetarian. Any salad dressing may be used, but to bring out the flavors in this salad, you may wish to use a light oil and balsamic vinegar or citrus dressing.

INGREDIENTS [2 servings]

1 head	*Lettuce*
1 lb.	*Salmon (optional), cooked*
1	*Orange, peeled and pith removed, cut into segments*
1	*Avocado, ripe, peeled, seed removed and cut into ½" slices*
½	*Red onion, quartered and sliced very thin*
2 tsp	*Sliced almonds*
4 oz.	*Goat cheese, crumbled*

COOKING INSTRUCTIONS

1. Simply place all ingredients on top of some lettuce, serving on individual plates.

GREEN SALAD WITH ORANGES, CRANBERRIES, PECANS

Another variation of a healthy green salad. This one pairs well with chicken. But if you wish to remain vegetarian or use it as a side salad, you can eliminate the meat. It pairs well with a light ranch dressing, but of course, use your favorite.

INGREDIENTS [2 servings]

1 head	*Lettuce*
1 lb.	*Chicken (optional) - tenders, browned and cooked*
1	*Orange, peeled and pith removed, cut into segments, then halved*
2 tbsp	*Dried cranberries*
2 tbsp	*Pecans, chopped*
2 tbsp	*Red onion, quartered and sliced very thin*
2 tbsp	*Gorgonzola cheese, crumbled*

COOKING INSTRUCTIONS

1. Simply place all ingredients on top of some lettuce, serving on individual plates.

PANZANELLA WITH HOME-MADE CROUTONS

One of the best reasons for growing cherry tomatoes is the enjoy their colors. Different colors bring a mix of flavors, with the yellow ones being mild, the orange exceptionally sweet, and the red having a burst of fresh sweet/acidic tomato flavor. A panzanella salad is a great way to use them, and it makes for a very pretty salad. It is also vegetarian. Add cooked shrimp to make it a main dish.

Home-made croutons are far better than the hard ones sold in stores and easy to make. (Plus, you can use gluten-free bread, which is harder to find as croutons.) They are good enough to eat alone as a snack!

PANZANELLA

INGREDIENTS [2 servings]

1 cup	*Colorful cherry tomatoes*
1 cup	*Cucumber, peeled, seeds removed, sliced in quarter pieces*
¼ cup	*Red onion, quartered and sliced very thin*
1 cup	*Mozzarella balls*
1 dozen	*Shrimp (optional), medium-large, deveined, tails removed, cooked*
1 tbsp	*Basil, dried or fresh*
½ cup	*Olive oil*

¼ cup	*Vinegar*
¼ cup	*Honey*
1 clove	*Garlic, minced*
½ tsp	*Salt*
1 cup	*Croutons (home-made recipe below)*
Sprigs	*Basil, fresh, for garnish*

1. Mix all ingredients in a bowl, except croutons and garnish.
2. Prior to serving, add croutons. Add fresh basil for a garnish.

HOME-MADE CROUTONS

INGREDIENTS

1 loaf	*French bread (best, but sandwich bread can also be used)*
2/3 cup	*Olive oil (amount may vary depending on size of bread loaf)*
1 clove	*Garlic (optional), minced*
1 tsp ea.	*Dried herbs - Basil, oregano, parsley, dill*
½ tsp	*Salt*

COOKING INSTRUCTIONS

1. Place olive oil and herbs in a large baggie and squeeze baggie until mixed. (This can also be done in a bowl.)
2. Slice and cut bread into ½" square cubes.
3. Add bread cubes to baggie and gently shake until each cube is thoroughly coated.
4. Place cubes on a cookie sheet.
5. In a pre-heated 350° convection oven or toaster oven, bake for approximately 10 minutes until lightly brown. If needed, use tongs to turn over each piece halfway through to brown the other side.

TOMATO AND CHEESE BISQUE

What to do with all those tomatoes that need picking? You can invest in canning, use them fresh in salads, or make soup! This recipe is an upscale version of tomato soup but it's easy to make.

The size of tomatoes will vary, affecting how many you need. Typically, Roma tomatoes, also known as Italian plum, are best used in soups, and on average four whole Roma tomatoes (2½ cups diced) equals 1 pound. If you do not have a lot of tomatoes on hand to use, you can buy canned tomatoes. And yes, if you do not wish to make soup from scratch, you can cheat further by buying your favorite brand of tomato soup as a base.

The secret to the flavor involves the spice bag. You will need a tea ball, empty tea bag, or cheesecloth to put the spices in. Heat up the soup with the spice bag, then add the cream and cheese.

INGREDIENTS [4 servings]

1, 28-oz. can or 2 lbs. (10-12) fresh	*Tomatoes, San Manzarino Roma (if possible)*
2 cups	*Vegetable broth*
4 tbsp	*Butter or olive oil*
½ cup	*Onion, diced*
3 cloves	*Garlic, crushed*
½ cup	*Shredded carrots*
1 cup	*Cheddar cheese*
½ cup	*Heavy cream*

1 tbsp	*Pickling spice*
½ tsp	*Salt*

COOKING INSTRUCTIONS

1. Slice and core tomatoes, then dice. Remove seeds if you wish. You do not need to remove the skins since they will be blended. But if you wish to anyway, dip tomatoes in boiling water for 30 seconds until the skins split, then place in cold water, and the skins should easily peel off. As mentioned, you can skip this entire step and start with a can of tomatoes if you prefer.
2. Melt butter or olive oil in a saucepan. Add onion, garlic, and carrot and sauté over medium heat until softened, approximately 5 minutes.
3. Add the tomatoes and the vegetable broth.
4. Place pickling spices in some sort of net, such as a tea ball, empty tea bag, or cheesecloth, and tie securely. Add to the saucepan.
5. Cook over medium heat for 20 minutes, stirring occasionally.
6. Remove the spice bag and set aside. Using a hand-held (immersion) blender, mix until smooth. If using a regular blender, blend the soup in batches, but it is a much messier method.
7. Add the spice bag back in. Cook for an additional 10 minutes. If your soup is too thick, add additional vegetable broth. If it is too thin, mix equal parts butter and flour in a saucepan, and cook until thickened - add a little bit at a time to your saucepan, stirring until the soup thickens to your preference level.
8. Remove the pan from the heat. Remove and discard the spice bag.
9. Stir in cheese, cream, and salt.
10. Garnish with chopped fresh basil, a few pieces of fresh diced tomatoes, a few cheese shreds, and, optionally, croutons.

TURKEY, BRIE, PEAR, MICROGREENS SANDWICH

Microgreens can be incorporated into healthy smoothies, sprinkled on top of a salad, placed on soups, or used as a garnish to make a dish look fancy. This recipe showcases another way to use them in a sandwich.

Some microgreens are spicier, while others are mild. Pay attention to the type of microgreen when buying or growing, and use the appropriate one for your specific dish. If you buy seeds or pre-mixed bags at the grocery store, the package will usually indicate "spicy mix." This recipe works best with a mild mix.

INGREDIENTS [2 sandwiches]

2	*Ciabatta rolls or focaccia bread, sliced*
¼ lb.	*Roasted sliced turkey*
4 oz.	*Brie cheese, pre-sliced if you can find it*
1	*Pear, peeled, sliced*
1 tbsp	*Mayonnaise*
1 tsp	*Honey mustard*
½ tsp	*Dill*
½ cup	*Microgreens*

COOKING INSTRUCTIONS

1. With luck, you can find brie cheese already sliced which is notoriously hard to do. If not, find the firmest one you can. Remove the white rind, then run a sharp knife under warm water and slice as thinly as possible.
2. Mix mayonnaise, honey mustard, and dill. Spread half of the mixture on the bottom half of the roll/bread.
3. Add turkey, pear, and brie, in that order, to the bottom half. Place the bottom half and the separated top half in a toaster oven. Broil until cheese is slightly melted but not messy. (The sole purpose of placing the top half in the oven also is to warm it.)
4. Remove from oven. Add microgreens on top of the cheese.
5. Spread the remaining half of the mayo/mustard mixture on the top half of the roll, and cover the sandwich.

SIDES

COLORFUL CARROT SALAD

Sometimes coleslaw is served so often as a side dish that it is nice to have something different. This salad can be used instead of coleslaw with meals and it looks especially pretty using colorful carrots.

INGREDIENTS [2 servings]

¼ cup each	*Carrots – orange, yellow/white, purple*
½ cup	*Raisins*
¼ cup	*Mayonnaise or olive oil, or a mix of both*
1 tsp	*Sour cream*

1. Shred carrots using the largest hole in your grater.
2. In a bowl combine carrots, raisins, and mayonnaise/oil, and mix.

COLORFUL SAUTEED CARROTS

Different colored carrots can be found in season in organic stores or at farmers' markets. If you cannot find them, use orange. Did you know that orange was not the original color of carrots? Purple was! Followed by yellow and white. Orange was developed to be a sweeter carrot. These are best cooked al dente.

INGREDIENTS [2 servings]

2 cups	*Carrots – orange, yellow/white, purple, cut into pieces*
2 tbsp	*Butter*
2 tbsp	*Thyme or dill, fresh*
1 tsp	*Sea salt*

COOKING INSTRUCTIONS

1. Slice carrots into thin pieces approximately 1" long.
2. Sautee over medium heat until al dente (or longer if you wish). Remove from heat.
3. Take sprigs of thyme and run your fingers down the stem, stripping the leaves off. If using dill, use culinary scissors to chop it.
4. Add thyme or dill leaves and salt to the warmed carrots.

CUBANELLA PEPPERS WITH CHEESE

I first learned of this recipe many years ago while camping with friends who shared it with us. The peppers were prepared as below but then wrapped in tin foil and cooked over the campfire. We have long since adapted it to indoor cooking. It is a great way to use this type of pepper without frying.

Use a mild flavored cheese rather than sharp to not overpower the peppers. Also, use white pepper if possible, which has a milder flavor than black.

INGREDIENTS [4 pieces]

2	*Cubanelle peppers*
½ cup	*Shredded Monterey Jack or mild white cheddar cheese*
½ tsp	*White pepper*

COOKING INSTRUCTIONS

1. Slice peppers in half and remove seeds and membranes.
2. Place on a dish to microwave on high for 30 seconds to soften slightly.
3. Arrange halves in a baking pan, interior sides up.
4. Sprinkle each with 2 tablespoons of the shredded cheese, filling the interior. Sprinkle with pepper.
5. Place in a pre-heated 350° toaster oven. Cook until the cheese is melted, approximately 3-5 minutes.

PEPPERS WITH THYME

Peppers can sometimes be cooked until they are mushy and overdone. This side dish cooks the peppers al dente (slightly firm). Simply using a good quality olive oil brings out the flavor of the peppers, and the thyme is a perfect aromatic accompaniment. And it is so pretty!

INGREDIENTS [2 servings]

1 each	*Bell peppers – red, orange, yellow*
1 tbsp	*Olive oil*
1 tbsp	*Thyme, preferably fresh*
½ tsp	*Salt*

COOKING INSTRUCTIONS

1. Cut peppers into slices approximately 3/8″ wide and 2″ long.
2. Heat olive oil over medium heat in a sauté pan.
3. Add peppers and stir to coat thoroughly with the olive oil.
4. Cover and cook for approximately 12 minutes, stirring occasionally. Remove from heat.
5. Strip fresh thyme from stems by running your finger down the stem. Add to peppers. (If using dried thyme, add it during the last minute of cooking to soften up.)
6. Sprinkle with salt.

ROASTED ACORN SQUASH

Acorn squash is typically thought of as a fall dish. But often you can find it in stores throughout the year. It makes a nice side dish, as in this recipe, but you can also stuff it with sausage and cheese to make a stand-alone meal.

INGREDIENTS [2 servings]

1	*Acorn squash*
4 tbsp	*Butter, sweet cream (unsalted)*
4 tbsp	*Brown sugar*
¼ tsp	*Nutmeg*

COOKING INSTRUCTIONS

1. Cut squash in half and remove center with seeds.
2. Place both halves, cut side up, on a cookie sheet in a pre-heated 375° oven. If they do not sit evenly balanced, you can cut a slice off the bottom, being careful not to cut through to the inside.
3. Cook until squash is tender, approximately 30 minutes, but time will vary depending on the size of your squash.
4. Top with butter and brown sugar on each half. Sprinkle with nutmeg.
5. This is the simplest way to prepare it, but you can also use your imagination to stuff the acorn squash with many other ingredients.

ROASTED BUTTERNUT SQUASH

There are so many wonderful dishes to create with butternut squash. You can mash it, adding butter and maple syrup. You can make it as a gratin with cream and cheese. You can make it as a soup (see separate recipe in this book). Or make this recipe for a sweet roasted version.

INGREDIENTS [4 servings]

16 oz.	*Butternut squash*
2 tbsp	*Olive oil*
¼ cup	*Butter, melted*
1 tsp	*Maple syrup*
½ tsp	*Nutmeg*
¼ tsp	*Cloves*
1 tsp	*Thyme, dried*
½ tsp	*Salt*

COOKING INSTRUCTIONS

1. Peel squash, cut in half, and remove center with seeds. Cut into cubes, approximately ¾".
2. Spread cubes evenly in a roasting pan. Add olive oil and coat the pieces thoroughly. This is sometimes done best by mixing in a bowl first before placing it in the pan.
3. Cook until squash is tender, approximately 30 minutes. Use a spatula to turn the squash pieces halfway through, if necessary, to brown. Or you may broil for 1-2 minutes to brown the pieces.
4. Place cooked squash in a bowl, then add butter, maple syrup, thyme, nutmeg, cloves, and salt.

ROASTED SPAGHETTI SQUASH

Spaghetti squash is a mild squash. It is sometimes used in place of pasta as a healthy and low-calorie alternative, covered with tomato sauce. However, it is wonderful with just butter and salt.

INGREDIENTS [4 servings]

1	*Spaghetti squash*
4 tbsp	*Butter, sweet cream (unsalted)*
1 tsp	*Parsley, cut*
½ tsp	*Salt*

COOKING INSTRUCTIONS

1. Cut squash in half and remove center with seeds.
2. Place both halves, cut side up, on a cookie sheet in a pre-heated 375° oven. If they do not sit evenly balanced, you can cut a slice off the bottom, being careful not to cut through to the inside.
3. Cook until squash is tender, approximately 60 minutes, but the time will vary depending on the size of your squash.
4. Remove squash from the skin with a fork. It will create "spaghetti" strands. Place in a serving dish.
5. When serving, top with plenty of butter. Add parsley for presentation.
6. Spaghetti squash is sumptuous when prepared simply like this. It is mild and tender, and butter is all you really need. However, many diets call for recipes using the strands as a low-calorie alternative to pasta, such as covering with tomato sauce.

TOMATO ASPIC

This gelatin-based vegetable side dish has a wonderful sweet and tart flavor to it. The cool, crunchy vegetables are great on a summer's day and very healthy, too.

My grandmother made this for years whenever we went to her home. Alas, with her passing, it fell by the wayside until I recently came across her recipe file while cleaning out my house.

Interestingly, the recipe called for ½ can of tomato soup. But there are so many brands and different can sizes nowadays. And most are ready to eat – you open the can and heat it up. So, what size/kind was meant for the recipe? Then I realized that back then, there was only one name in the soup business, and that was Campbell's brand. And it was condensed, meaning you had to add the water yourself before heating. And then, I was able to convert what "½ can" meant in terms of ounces.

I have since made this recipe myself and still love the interesting flavor mix. Making it again has brought back fond memories of good food and great times. Hopefully, you will enjoy it as well.

INGREDIENTS [4 servings]

½ cup	*Tomato soup, condensed + ½ cup water OR*
	1 cup of ready-made tomato soup already constituted
½ cup	*Chili sauce*
2 tbsp	*Water*
2 pkgs	*Unflavored gelatin*
1 tbsp	*White vinegar*
1 tbsp	*Lemon juice*

½ c.	*Sugar*
½ cup	*Onion, white, diced*
½ cup	*Celery, diced*
½ cup	*Pepper, green*
Dash	*Cloves*
Leaves	*Lettuce, red, for garnish*

COOKING INSTRUCTIONS

1. Combine the tomato soup and ½ cup water (or ready-made tomato soup), and chili sauce in a pan and bring to a boil. Remove from heat.
2. Meanwhile, dissolve gelatin in 2 tablespoons of water.
3. Add vinegar and lemon juice to gelatin.
4. Combine soup/chili sauce and gelatin mix in a bowl. Let sit in the refrigerator for 3 hours (or in the freezer for 1 hour) until partially set.
5. Stir in remaining INGREDIENTS vegetables, sugar, cloves.
6. Pour into individual molds if you have them; otherwise, use muffin tins. Continue to refrigerate until completely set, approximately 1 hour.
7. For serving, remove from mold and place atop lettuce.

EPILOGUE

Eating healthy and naturally is in. Happy growing and cooking!

ABOUT THE AUTHOR

Rondi is a horticulturist and Florida master gardener. For two decades she worked in the horticultural field, including at various local garden centers as a grower and seller of plants, as a grower of organic herb and vegetable plants in her own greenhouses for farmers' markets, and by providing on-site consultations for landscape design and plant diagnostics.

As a master gardener coordinator, she taught future enthusiasts the knack of gardening. And she has been teaching gardening locally for over a decade. She is also the chairperson of the Landscape & Garden Club for her community.

She resides in The Villages, Florida, with her husband and menagerie of pets, surrounded by her tropical oasis of plants, gardens, and natural woods.

Made in the USA
Coppell, TX
30 June 2026

83828479R00098